Lyle's latest work, *Easy to Follow: Leadership by following in the footsteps of Christ*, exemplifies the notion that smart people have a knack for making the complicated simple. It's not enough, however, to say that his work lives up to its title; it's also chock-full of the values that our own company abides by—it's playful, disruptive, intimate, and authentic. What more could you ask for? To become a better person? It might just help you with that, too!

Mark Sourian, president of production at 5&2 Studios (*The Chosen* series)

The leadership world is a crowded and busy space. Often you can be overwhelmed by all the noise, pitches, and gimmicks that promise big and perform small. Lyle and the team at Integrus Leadership are the opposite. They move the needle for those who have the courage and desire to grow and change. Their work has been transformational for Cornerstone Church and Hagee Ministries and for me personally. The fundamental truths and proven principles that Lyle brings to the forefront create a clear path for leaders to follow. In the complicated and complex leadership journey you face, allow Lyle to serve you. He's a thoughtful and courageous guide helping navigate the difficult route from where you are to where you are called to be. In *Easy to Follow* Lyle provides a powerful picture of what we should all strive for as leaders and followers of Christ—and a reminder that we still have work to do. Some books you read, and other books read you. The work you hold in your hand is indeed a place to study what it means to lead like Jesus.

Matthew Hagee, lead pastor of Cornerstone Church

Lyle Wells and Kat Armstrong team up to present a fresh vantage point on being a Christlike leader. In *Easy to Follow*, you'll discover the nuances that separate toxic leadership behaviors from the ways of Jesus. Self-evaluation abounds, and they leave margin for it to happen. You'll find clear distinctions in leadership practices and the mindset shifts that align you more with Jesus. Every chapter reinforces key principles through personal reflection, team discussion questions, and invitations for team feedback. They've made transferring insights from head to heart to action easy! I highly recommend this book to anyone who longs to become more like Jesus and will commit to following his lead.

Tami Heim, president and CEO of Christian Leadership Alliance

Leaders are learners. The moment you stop learning you forfeit the right to lead. One of the ways I have been privileged to learn is through a coaching relationship with Lyle Wells. My life and my leadership have been influenced beyond words. I am so thankful for *Easy to Follow*, which will allow leaders everywhere to learn from his wisdom and counsel. Lyle's biblical approach to leadership, combined with his years of experience as both a leader and a developer of leaders, will challenge you in ways you cannot imagine. I am excited about this book and the impact it will have in the lives of learning leaders everywhere!

Vance Pitman, president of Send Network and author of *The Stressless Life* and *Unburdened*

In a time plagued by failures of leadership in the body of Christ, *Easy to Follow* doesn't let us lose hope. It's an invitation to refocus our attention on the basics of emulating the life of Christ as we pursue health. This book is timely, insightful, and practical for leaders and laypeople alike.

Tanner Peake, president and CEO of Every Home for Christ

In *Easy to Follow*, Lyle Wells masterfully blends profound insights with practical guidance, inviting leaders on a transformative journey toward authentic leadership rooted in the teachings of Jesus. Each chapter serves as a beacon for those seeking to escape the pitfalls of toxic leadership and embrace a style that inspires, uplifts, and connects.

I have personally benefited from Lyle's extensive experience as a mentor and coach, so it is no surprise that in this text he challenges us to move beyond mere management to genuine mentorship. His compelling call to action—"Are you easy to follow?"—encourages us to reflect on our own leadership practices and their impact on our teams.

This book is not just for those in positions of authority but for anyone striving to lead with integrity and purpose. Lyle's insights will empower you to cultivate an environment where generosity and collaboration thrive. Whether you're a seasoned leader or just beginning your journey, *Easy to Follow* is an essential read that will enrich your perspective and equip you to lead with faith and authenticity.

Brandon Cormier, lead pastor of Zeal Church

In *Easy to Follow*, Lyle Wells and Kat Armstrong provide a Jesus-centered, character-based antidote to the leadership models and advice that have proven harmful to so many individuals and organizations in recent years. If you follow the guidelines in this book, you will become a better leader not merely by improving your skills but by becoming a better *person* who implements those skills.

Angie Ward, PhD, director of the doctor of ministry program and associate professor of leadership and ministry at Denver Seminary

TRADING TOXIC LEADERSHIP
for the WAY OF JESUS

EASY TO FOLLOW

LYLE WELLS
with KAT ARMSTRONG

Published in alliance with
Tyndale House Publishers

NavPress.com

Easy to Follow: Trading Toxic Leadership for the Way of Jesus

Copyright © 2025 by Integrus Leadership. All rights reserved.

lylewells.com
integrus.org

A NavPress resource published in alliance with Tyndale House Publishers

NavPress is a registered trademark of NavPress, The Navigators, Colorado Springs, CO, registered in the United States of America. The NavPress logo is a trademark of NavPress, The Navigators, Colorado Springs, CO. *Tyndale* is a registered trademark of Tyndale House Ministries, registered in the United States of America. Absence of ® in connection with marks of NavPress or other parties does not indicate an absence of registration of those marks.

The Team: David Zimmerman, Publisher; Caitlyn Carlson, Senior Editor; Elizabeth Schroll, Copyeditor; Lacie Phillips, Production Assistant; Tim Green, Cover Designer; Cathy Miller, Interior Designer; Sarah Ocenasek, Proofreading Coordinator

Cover design by Faceout Studio

Cover and interior illustration of houndstooth pattern copyright © by Bobnevv/Shutterstock. All rights reserved.

Lyle Wells photo copyright © 2023 by Ashley Monogue. All rights reserved.
Kat Armstrong photo copyright © 2023 by Dyan Kethley. All rights reserved.

All Scripture quotations, unless otherwise indicated, are taken from the Holy Bible, *New International Version*,® *NIV*.® Copyright © 1973, 1978, 1984, 2011 by Biblica, Inc.® Used by permission. All rights reserved worldwide. Scripture quotations marked CSB are taken from the Christian Standard Bible,® copyright © 2017 by Holman Bible Publishers. Used by permission. Christian Standard Bible® and CSB® are federally registered trademarks of Holman Bible Publishers. Scripture quotation marked HCSB is taken from the Holman Christian Standard Bible,® copyright © 1999, 2000, 2002, 2003, 2009 by Holman Bible Publishers. Used by permission. Holman Christian Standard Bible,® Holman CSB,® and HCSB® are federally registered trademarks of Holman Bible Publishers. Scripture quotation marked KJV is taken from the *Holy Bible*, King James Version. Scripture quotation marked NET is taken from the New English Translation, NET Bible,® copyright ©1996–2006 by Biblical Studies Press, L.L.C. http://netbible.com. All rights reserved. Scripture quotations marked NLT are taken from the *Holy Bible*, New Living Translation, copyright © 1996, 2004, 2015 by Tyndale House Foundation. Used by permission of Tyndale House Publishers, Carol Stream, Illinois 60188. All rights reserved. Scripture quotations marked NRSV are taken from the New Revised Standard Version Bible, copyright © 1989 National Council of the Churches of Christ in the United States of America. Used by permission. All rights reserved worldwide.

Some of the anecdotal illustrations in this book are true to life and are included with the permission of the persons involved. All other illustrations are composites of real situations, and any resemblance to people living or dead is purely coincidental.

For information about special discounts for bulk purchases, please contact Tyndale House Publishers at csresponse@tyndale.com, or call 1-855-277-9400.

ISBN 978-1-64158-942-0

Printed in the United States of America

31	30	29	28	27	26	25
7	6	5	4	3	2	1

LYLE: *For Flip and Susan,
the easiest-to-follow leaders I've ever known.*

KAT: *For Caleb Armstrong.
You're becoming an easy-to-follow leader.*

Contents

	Foreword by John Bevere *xi*
INTRODUCTION	Hard to Follow? *1*
ONE	Jesus Is Easy to Follow *5*
TWO	Jesus Clearly Defined His Mission *19*
THREE	Jesus Taught His Methods; He Didn't Just Tell Them *43*
FOUR	Jesus Mentored, Not Managed, His Team *59*
FIVE	Jesus Practiced Uncommon Compassion *73*
SIX	Jesus Clarified His Expectations *91*
SEVEN	Jesus Cultivated Generosity *103*
EIGHT	Jesus Empowered Others *119*
A FINAL QUESTION	Are You Easy to Follow? *133*

Acknowledgments *139*
Resources for Leaders *141*
Integrus Leadership Resources *143*
About the Authors *145*
Notes *147*

Foreword

Easy to follow. I wish this were true of all leaders. But sadly, it isn't. As someone who served in two ministries before I began to lead my own, traveling to over one thousand churches in thirty-five years and speaking to many leadership groups, I've experienced and witnessed the tragedy of following toxic leaders. The crushing burden of these chaotic environments doesn't just make the work difficult—often it causes those who are under this form of leadership to question themselves, their abilities, and even their callings.

The story of Saul and David offers us a striking contrast between toxic and healthy leadership. Saul was riddled with insecurity and sought validation through people pleasing rather than pursuing the glory of God. His thirst for recognition and control led him to view David—a loyal servant—as a threat. Saul's leadership was marked by insecurity, which led to jealousy, fear, and self-preservation, which ultimately became his downfall.

David, on the other hand, demonstrated a different approach. Grounded in his relationship with God, David maintained a pure and faithful heart, even when surrounded by severe dysfunction. He refused to let Saul's broken leadership define him. Instead, David trusted God's timing and justice, leading with humility and reliance on God's strength. Because of this, God honored David, entrusting him with great responsibility, influence, and a legacy that continues to inspire.

Their stories challenge us to reflect on our own leadership and the environments we foster. Are we leading like Saul, driven by insecurity and self-interest, or are we striving to lead like David, rooted in holy fear and humility?

I'm grateful that my dear friend Lyle Wells has written this book. Very few leaders carry the character and competence to lead with ease that Lyle does. For several years now, he has coached me and my team, helping us create a culture where others can flourish as they answer the call to follow. Lyle has not only helped us scale as an organization but also equipped us to navigate some challenging team dynamics and situations. I have absolute confidence he'll do the same for you!

Every leader has the potential to be *easy to follow*. That doesn't mean leadership is easy; it means that great leaders create clarity, empower others, and cultivate cultures where people thrive. In this book, Lyle explores practical ways to embody the kind of leadership that reflects the heart of Jesus, the greatest leader of all time.

Jesus' simple invitation—"Follow me"—launched the most transformative movement in history. His leadership wasn't about gaining power, control, or domination over others but about living for a cause greater than himself, one where greatness is found in serving others, making room for them to contribute and to flourish in their God-given callings and giftings.

Leadership is a sacred trust, a calling to steward the time, talents, and energy of those we serve. Whether you're leading a team of two or a movement of millions, the principles in this book will help you become a leader who is not only worth following but also easy to follow.

John Bevere
bestselling author and minister
cofounder of Messenger International and MessengerX

INTRODUCTION
HARD TO FOLLOW?

Demoralized. I never want any leader to feel that way—because I know what it's like.

I would start every day with my routines of prayer, quiet time, and exercise, thinking the entire time, *Today's the day; it's going to be different today.* But it never was.

Serving as a leader at this massive Christian organization was a grind. Years after I left, the senior leader made headlines for bullying and was ousted by the board, who said he was biblically disqualified from leadership.

During this season of leadership, I turned to grim humor to cope with the toxic work environment. I used to joke that I felt like a dog named Stay who was constantly given the contradictory command to "come." "Come, Stay!" If I acted deliberately and prudently, I'd be in trouble for not acting decisively or immediately. When I responded quickly or aggressively, I'd get criticized for acting too quickly or without good judgment. The resulting whiplash caused me to question two things: my ability to lead and my calling as a leader.

What's wrong with me? I wondered. I was obviously not hitting the mark, and that was disorienting because up until this point in my life as a leader, I'd hit the mark everywhere I'd served. Doubting my ability to lead created the second nagging question: *Am I called to do this?*

From my first day on the job until the day I resigned, a week hardly went by without some sort of crisis involving the senior leader. He'd ruthlessly criticize downline leaders for failing to live up to a standard that was rarely communicated or for being generally incompetent. Shaming and condemnation—often showing up in demeaning comments like "We shouldn't have sent a boy to do a man's job"—were common.

Why would I choose to work in this toxic environment? Well, the organization's mission was compelling. To this day, I'm convinced we were positioned to catalyze revival in North America. And even knowing that I'd be dealing with a leader who wasn't easy to follow, I thought I could change things. Never could I have imagined that my role would primarily involve not mobilizing leaders and resources to spark a movement of God but reining in a loose cannon. We had a massive reach and enviable resources, but we lacked a culture where people felt valued, empowered, and fully equipped to pursue the mission of the organization.

Trust me: I'm good with hard. If I know who my enemies are

and where the challenges are coming from, I can deal with that. But when your enemies are your leaders, when the people who are supposed to provide clarity and encouragement are doing the opposite, it makes you want to throw in the towel. That's not the kind of leadership culture God wants his people to experience. God is not cruel; he doesn't throw us into confusion.

What makes a leader hard to follow isn't usually one or two big things. It's all the little things that add up—death by a thousand cuts. It's the lack of clarity, the multitude of priorities that few can define and no one can rank. It's the mixed messages that come from being told what to do and how to do it and then being chastised for doing it that way and not using your own judgment or experience. It's the feeling of constant failure that comes from the criticality of people who point out others' mistakes as a way of shielding themselves from harsh evaluation by the leader. Trade clarity for confusion, unity for self-preservation, and purpose for survival, and you will see a culture turn toxic in very short measure.

If you've experienced that kind of leadership, you know how draining and demoralizing it is. Hear me on this: Even when the mission and outcomes are noteworthy, the damage done to those who work under toxic leaders, and consequently their families, undermines all the good. A hard-to-follow leader is never worth the cost.

But it doesn't have to be this way.

I have the privilege of engaging with thousands of leaders in hundreds of faith-forward organizations. I see their passion, their zeal, their talent. What a great responsibility we carry as leaders to steward the time and talents of those we serve. How can we learn, grow, and develop into leaders who serve them well? My answer to this question was to turn to the leader who has created the greatest movement in the history of the world, the man with billions of people who claim to be his followers, the one who started it all with two simple words: *Follow me*.

ONE
JESUS IS EASY TO FOLLOW

"Whoever wants to be great among you must be your servant."
JESUS (MATTHEW 20:26, NET)

Did you know that the Bible never calls Jesus a leader?

Of course, we know that Jesus is the greatest leader who ever lived. But in the Gospels, the word *lead* is rarely used in reference to Jesus. In the descriptions of events like the visits to Caesarea Philippi and to Gethsemane, the Bible states that Jesus and the disciples "went" to these destinations. We know through context that these destinations were intentionally selected by Jesus, yet Scripture doesn't say that Jesus led the disciples to them. When Jesus led, people willingly surrendered their lives and their livelihoods to follow him wherever he was going. Even if it came at a great cost or inconvenience.

Jesus was the kind of leader who could extend an invitation to someone to vacate their home, leave their profession, and desert their way of life, and they would make following him their sole mission. Jesus didn't proclaim himself a leader. He traveled and talked and healed and taught, and people moved toward him.

Jesus was so compelling that his *very presence* led people.

Matthew abandoned his highly profitable tollbooth to follow him.

Mary of Bethany poured out her expensive perfume to anoint his feet.

Peter lunged toward armed Roman guards with a sword to defend him.

Jesus could motion to his disciples to move one way, and they'd jump to their feet to pursue their Savior. He didn't lead with an iron fist; he didn't bully his followers or pressure them with force. Jesus led in a countercultural way that ignited a movement that's still alive and well today. Reborn into his love, men and women were willing to follow wherever their Lord led—even after his resurrection and return to his Father's side. Christ followers were willing to surrender comfort, willing to deny privileges, willing to reject their social status, willing to give it all, even their livelihood and their lives, for the cause of Christ.

Over the centuries, even as Christ followers faced persecution, disruption, and the failures of the church, people continued to follow him. People still choose to follow Jesus every day.

So how is it that a Jewish carpenter from Bethlehem managed to ignite a spiritual revolution—a global religious movement? How did Jesus compel his disciples to follow him to the Cross? To be willing to die for the cause of Christ? What was it about Jesus that motivated the radical conversion of his contemporaries? Why did they abandon their former way of life and embrace a new, uncharted course?

Jesus was easy to follow. That's how. That's why.

Now, I know that might sound reductionistic. Obviously, Jesus' leadership effectiveness is grounded in his deity. He is the Son of God,[1] the promised Messiah,[2] the King of all kings and Lord of all lords.[3] But while Jesus is 100 percent God, he is also 100 percent human. Which means that as humans who bear the image of God to the world we are not just called but also *created* to lead like Jesus.

When we choose to follow Jesus, we *become* new people, and we *are becoming* new people. Which is not to say that becoming an easy-to-follow leader is easy. Following Jesus' example will be the greatest challenge of our lives. But a relationship with Jesus frees us from slavery to sin, and our outward lives begin to match our inward redemption: Our motivations change, our behaviors change, and the entirety of our being orbits around the life, death, and resurrection of Christ. As a result, we live and lead differently when we know Jesus as our Savior. Or we should, shouldn't we?

That's what this book is all about: leading like Jesus. It's about following Jesus so closely, so intently, that we practice Christlikeness with all our hearts, souls, minds, and strength and become easy to follow like Jesus.

You may not think it's possible to lead like Jesus. But I want to challenge you that it's part of the very definition of becoming Christlike. As we allow Jesus to conform our hearts, souls, minds, and strength to his work and ways, as we continue to follow wherever he leads, we will find ourselves reflecting who he is not just in our personal lives but also as leaders. And as we do, we will discover something profound: Becoming like Jesus means that we, too, become easy to follow.

AN EASY-TO-FOLLOW LEADER

When I was an emerging leader, early in my career, my passion would get the best of me; instead of helping people discover their purpose, I'd attempt to *drive* others toward our desired outcomes. I used tactics I learned from secular leadership books that focused on power, authority, and positional influence—but that involved using fear, intimidation, and threats to achieve my purposes, all in the name of serving others. I was not a leader who was easy to follow. Often, my ungodly actions were successful in achieving my objectives and the organization's goals, but good metrics are not God's only measure of good leadership.

Then I decided to use a Bible concordance to investigate what the Scriptures teach about leadership. That's when I discovered, to my shock, that *leadership* isn't a word used often in the Bible. Jesus never identified himself as a leader; he simply invited people to follow. Jesus didn't drive his disciples to surrender their lives; he simply directed them to. Jesus let his life lead his original disciples, along with countless others, to a life of purpose, provision, and promise.

Unfortunately, like me in my early leadership days, many Christians try to adapt secular leadership training to their sacred calling to lead. The problem with this method is that most leadership direction focuses solely on results—and sometimes results at any cost, or results that come with collateral damage. Sadly, we've just accepted this as the cost of doing ministry or Kingdom-focused business. But nothing could be further from the truth. We're not supposed to shrug off the "bodies behind the bus."

You and I are called by God to be like Jesus. We're called to lead like Jesus. To be easy to follow, not hard to endure.

The real goal in our leadership should not be to look like a better leader; it should be to *be a leader who looks like Jesus*. And to do that, we have to face the mirror and examine our reflections unflinchingly. We must stare down our current leadership practices and peer past what we think our leadership should look like. We know we're becoming easy to follow when we see something a little more like Christ's reflection looking back at us when we look at ourselves.

If we don't see Christ in the mirror yet, that means we'll have to change. There's no way around it. Some of us may need to make some small pivots in the way we lead others. Others might require a 180-degree rotation—an about-face. But it will be worth it.

What made Jesus easy to follow probably wasn't that he adhered to popular leadership advice you've received in the past. You will need courage and conviction to choose the way of Jesus, especially when it goes against your favorite leadership book, your go-to leadership podcast, or a leader you look up to because of their success. When Jesus disagrees with your leadership training, it's time to abandon the wisdom of people and embrace the example of Christ.

REDEFINING LEADERSHIP

I used to believe that a leader was anyone who set a course. That's why early in my life I wanted to be a leader—because I wanted a voice, and sometimes a vote, in the course I was traveling. As a high school student, I ran for student-council offices, was a captain on athletic teams, and even enrolled in management classes for my part-time job. I embraced a sled dog–team metaphor: If you aren't the lead dog, then the scenery won't change much.

Now, with decades of leadership experience under my belt, I know that that definition of leadership is incomplete at best: Not all leaders set courses. Yes, leadership from the top is crucial to organizational alignment, but just as important are the leadership behaviors of everyone else on a team. Some of the most effective leaders carry out the course that has already been set.

The Bellagio hotel in Las Vegas is one of the top tourist destinations in the world and is considered the standard when it comes to hospitality and customer service. I experienced that for myself a few years ago when I was there to facilitate a workshop. Stepping into their beautiful lobby is a delightful and overwhelming experience. The Bellagio takes up 4.2 million square feet, and I needed to find a specific conference room. I approached a bellman and asked him to point me toward the room on my itinerary. He simply said, "Follow me." I quickly replied that he didn't need to take me to my destination—that I was fully capable of following directions—but he insisted on taking me. As we wound our way through rows of slot machines, around crap tables, and past dozens of restaurants, he explained to me that part of their five-star service commitment is to always *take* people to a destination rather than simply *tell* them how to get there.

Leadership is not a title or a personality type. It is behavior that influences others and drives outcomes. Which means we are all leading. Whether you are the CEO of a large corporation or a leader at a church; whether you work for a nonprofit or own your own business; whether you are a parent or a student or a teacher—you are a leader. Leadership isn't a special gift for a select few but a practice that everyone can embrace and anyone can fortify.

As I matured, I embraced this larger definition of leadership: Leadership is behavior that influences others. Influence can be positive or negative—that is, although this definition applies to leaders I admire, like Billy Graham, it also applies to those who use their influence to harm others. Some of the most destructive leaders coerce their followers into obedience. That's why leadership for a Kingdom-minded leader can't just be about influence.

So if we are all leading and all have some kind of influence—what behaviors are we exhibiting, and what results are they creating?

As a pastor, I strive to leverage my credibility, influence, and skills to help people find and follow Jesus; I want to take them from a place where they are lost, languishing, hurting, and hopeless to the peaceful and purposeful life of a Christ follower. In my role as a leader of leaders at Integrus Leadership, where we focus on behavior leadership through executive coaching and leadership training, I aim to identify and eliminate the personal and organizational constraints that leave many Christian leaders feeling both stuck and scared. In every space I lead, I'm living out this deeply held belief: If leadership is not about others, it's broken.

When I lead workshops, I frequently ask participants to name a movie that exemplifies outstanding leadership. As people start shouting out examples, I raise the stakes: There is a reward for the person who can guess my favorite leadership movie. After about ninety seconds of chaos (and never the answer I am looking for), I shock them by revealing my all-time favorite leadership movie: *Cinderella*. Think about it—the fairy godmother, with no agenda of her own, shows up and facilitates a path for Cinderella to move from where she is to where she dreams and desires to go. What a leader!

Some leaders would tell you that there are two great days in a person's life: the day you are born and the day you discover your purpose on earth. I would add a third great day: the day you show up to help someone not just know their purpose but also pursue it.

FOLLOW ME AS I FOLLOW CHRIST

My dad died when I was six years old, but I still have vivid memories of him more than fifty years later. I loved my father. I loved him so much that I wanted to be just like him. I wanted to do everything just the way my dad did it.

When I was a toddler, I'd tag along with my dad to work as he supported other farmers in his co-op. If he had work to do, you'd better believe I was right by his side. If he needed to make a delivery, my full attention would be on watching him drop off fuel and supplies to hardworking, salt-of-the-earth men and women. If he wore sunglasses, I wanted to wear sunglasses. If he took them off, I'd take mine off. If he spit, I spit. (I guess you could say I wanted to be his spitting image.)

Being a copycat can certainly express our admiration of someone, but it can also significantly benefit us when we are emulating people worthy of that honor. In my teenage years I developed a friendship with Wendall Williams, a teammate two years older than me who embodied high character, set lofty goals, lived with integrity, and had a zealous work ethic. Wendall was the perfect template for me in those years—a great friend who could have a lot of fun but also knew when to focus and work toward high-value goals.

When I graduated from college and began my career as an educator, I started to emulate a leader named Dominic Capra. Dominic was a leader with great presence and focus, and he loved his wife well and treated his children with tenderness. By God's grace, he mentored me and started influencing my view of leadership when I was still impressionable. His love for Christ, his commitment to his family, and the way he invested in me set me on a course I'm still on today.

You see, we're always learning our leadership practices from someone. Maybe it is a parent, a role model, a friend, or a mentor. But we are all being shaped into leaders. As such, we need to ask a key question: *Whom are we imitating in our leadership?* Is it Jesus? Or have we relegated Jesus' example to the "spiritual" parts of our ministry and Kingdom work?

My prayer for you, as you read this book, is that you will elevate Jesus as your ultimate example for leading well and then align your own leadership with the way of Christ. Whether you are on the brink of a new position of influence or a veteran leader looking to take a new step of leadership, these pages will equip you with simple resources to lead like Jesus.

In the next seven chapters, I'll guide you through seven principles that highlight Jesus' leadership practices. We'll discover that Jesus led his mission with leadership qualities that are often undervalued in our society—like clarity, mentorship, empathy, and generosity. I'll help you see how the Scriptures call attention to Jesus' method of influencing his disciples, and then I'll offer you practical recommendations to begin practicing these principles with your team.

When I use the language of "your team" throughout this book, I'm not necessarily talking about a team who reports to you or a team you oversee (although that may be the case). Your team is the group of leaders you are part of—the context where you have influence, whether it's part of an official role or not. What you do on a team or in an organization may change, but Jesus' leadership posture will apply to every role you'll ever hold.

My hope is that each chapter will be so life-changing that just the words on the page will catalyze you to action. But I also know that most of the time when a message resonates with us, we need time for further reflection, and we need a group of other leaders to hold us accountable to make the change we're seeking. That's why I've included three or four personal reflection questions at the end of each chapter, three team discussion questions, and three questions you can use to invite feedback into your life. You can also use this QR code to find the *Easy to Follow* guide, which includes the questions from each chapter as well as prayer prompts and journaling space.

I know this is a bold move. But I'm going to ask for your trust. I'll ask that you follow me as I follow Christ. Not because I've perfected being easy to follow. Just ask my team; I'm a work in progress. But I've been devoted to Christlike behavioral leadership for decades. I've worked with thousands of catalytic leaders like you, and I know what kind of support you need to see growth in your leadership skills.

You're going to need my vulnerability, and you'll have it. I won't skirt around my own failings. I'll share the lessons I've learned without leaving out the parts where I've messed up. I want you to be able to jump over hurdles that have tripped me up.

You'll need me to tell you what you need to know quickly, because you've got innumerable responsibilities. I won't mince words; I'll get straight to the point. But I'll always leave you with the next steps so you aren't just thinking about growing and changing; you'll actually change. It has been said that when you know better you do better. But I believe when you *do* better you actually do better.

And last, you'll need the Holy Spirit's power to be easy to follow. I've spent hours praying for every person who opens this book. Know this: God wants to catalyze you for Kingdom work. He's called you, so he will equip you.

We can't do this on our own. A willing spirit won't be enough. This is a *holy* endeavor, so it requires a *Holy* Spirit. The good news is that if you follow Jesus the Spirit of God is already at work in your life, and he wants to transform your leadership so that you reflect Christ to everyone you serve and to all you influence.

PERSONAL REFLECTION QUESTIONS
Write out your answers before you go to bed tonight.

1. Who have been the leadership models and mentors in my life? What did they teach me well? What bad habits have I learned that I need to address?

2. Who has led me and been easy to follow? What specific characteristics do I notice that contributed to a healthy leadership environment? Do I demonstrate those qualities in my leadership today?

3. Who has led me and been hard to follow? What specific characteristics do I notice that contributed to a toxic leadership environment? Do I display any of those traits in my leadership now?

TEAM DISCUSSION QUESTIONS

Ask these questions during your next team meeting.

1. When have you felt well led? What did that look like?
2. Give a couple of examples of leaders, besides Jesus, whom you would describe as easy to follow.
3. If you had been one of Jesus' original disciples, which aspect of his leadership do you think would have been most encouraging to you?

INVITATIONAL QUESTIONS FOR FEEDBACK

Using one of these questions, ask at least one person you lead for feedback in the next seven days.

1. Do you feel heard and seen by me in my leadership role?
2. Are my communication rhythms and check-ins serving you well?
3. What are your short-term and long-term goals for your current role?

TWO

JESUS CLEARLY DEFINED HIS MISSION

"The Son of Man came to seek and to save the lost."
JESUS (LUKE 19:10)

One of the bestselling books in my lifetime has been Rick Warren's *The Purpose Driven Life*. Its message has resonated with people so deeply that this book has been distributed on every continent and in nearly every country, selling fifty million copies in 137 languages.[1] Billions of people are searching for their purpose—a mission that drives their life and defines their existence. As humans, we understand this truth innately: that a life without true purpose is lost, and a lost life is a wasted life.

A man named John Harper has a thing or two to teach us about purpose. John Harper was born in the late 1800s in Scotland, and four short years after converting to Christianity at the age of fourteen, he embraced a call to ministry. As a young man, he was planted as the first pastor of a new congregation in Glasgow, where he became well-known for his preaching.

In 1911 the Moody Church in Chicago invited Harper to come to America and preach for several weeks. When he was invited to come back the following year, he accepted. Harper, a widower, was joined by his six-year-old daughter and his sister in April of 1912 as he stepped aboard the *Titanic*.

After the ship struck the iceberg and the passengers realized that their boat had become incapacitated, Harper secured his daughter and sister into a lifeboat—and then returned to the deck to preach the gospel to the passengers who remained on the ship. As the boat started to descend into the Atlantic, he grabbed a life jacket and continued to witness to the masses now doomed in the freezing waters.

John Harper's final moment came shortly after he encountered a man floating near him in the water. Harper asked the man if he knew Jesus Christ as Lord, and the man replied that he didn't. Harper declared Acts 16:31: "Believe in the Lord Jesus, and you will be saved." Later, Harper removed his life jacket and gave it to another person, saying, "You need this more than I do!" and disappearing into the depths of the icy sea. The man Harper had witnessed to was later pulled into a lifeboat and survived. He came forward following the rescue operation to share his story, declare his faith, and confirm that he was John Harper's last convert.[2]

John Harper was just shy of his fortieth birthday, and he died as he had lived since receiving the call to preach at eighteen: on mission to preach the gospel. Can you imagine having a mission so compelling, so much a part of your core, that you fulfill it even in the very last hours of your life? A mission that means so much to you that you are willing to surrender your very life? John Harper was a mission-minded man. He knew his purpose and lived it out, however extreme the circumstances became.

How about you? If you knew that your lifespan would be measured not in months or years but hours, how would you respond? Would you seek pleasure or one last experience of self-indulgence? Or do you have a passion that burns so hot that it would compel you to pursue it until you take your final breath?

WHY MISSION?

In the early days of Integrus, the company I lead that serves Kingdom-minded leaders and their teams, we juggled a myriad of priorities. We needed to serve leaders, create compelling content, build our brand, define our target audience, and make enough money to pay our bills. Our organization struggled for the first few years as we tried to meet these needs and define our mission.

I had to learn a hard lesson: that without a clearly defined mission our efforts are compromised, our focus is diluted, and our impact is negated.

Sometimes we miss the simplest, most effective way to lead because we don't read familiar Bible stories with the intent of discovering *how* Jesus went about fulfilling his mission. When we do, here's what we'll find: Being an easy-to-follow leader requires first clearly defining our mission.

When I say "our mission," I'm actually not talking about your organization's vision statement or what your church does to reach the community. I'm talking about you specifically. Mission always starts with the leader. Your mission is your personality, giftings, and passions all directed into focused action. If you don't have clarity on what God built you to do and how he wants you to do it, you'll have a hard time leading people toward effective mission as a team.

Have you ever completed a personal mission statement or made a mission statement for your family? If you have created a mission statement before, how often do you reflect on it and measure your work and your leadership through its lens? Is there a chance you might be taking it for granted?

I know many of us are familiar with mission statements. But in my line of work I often meet leaders who are spread thin, distracted, and reactive. Mission drift happens far more easily and quietly than we might expect.

If you've lost sight of your passion, you've forgotten why you're on mission. If you're coasting through each day or plugging along to get through the workday without intentionally considering what your contribution is and how it's part of the whole, you're missing out on the Lord's best for you, the people you love, and the people you work with.

In those early days of trying to sort through the priorities and mission for Integrus, I found myself studying Deuteronomy 3. When I came across verse 28, where the Lord commands Moses to "encourage and strengthen" Joshua, the light came on. Years of floundering and frustration were eliminated when our leadership team determined that we existed solely to encourage and strengthen faith-based leaders.

Identifying our purpose proved vital for leading Integrus into long-term sustainability for three key reasons:

1. We were able to **prioritize our actions and align our resources** toward our goal. We focused on creating content that would uplift and equip leaders, building our

brand as a trusted resource in the faith-based leadership community and targeting our marketing efforts toward this specific audience.

2. Having a clear mission also **brought clarity to our decision-making process.** We could easily evaluate whether an opportunity or initiative aligned with our purpose and whether it would help us serve faith-based leaders. This helped us prioritize our resources and say no to distractions that would divert us from our mission.

3. Having a clearly defined mission **gave our organization a sense of direction and purpose.** The mission became a rallying point for our team and helped us stay focused and motivated during challenging times. We knew that every effort we made was contributing to strengthening and encouraging faith-based leaders, and that gave us a sense of fulfillment and purpose.

If I'd been paying attention to Jesus' mission statement, maybe I would have thought to create more focus earlier in my career as a leader. I'm grateful I figured it out quickly enough to help set a clear and healthy course for Integrus. And I hope you learn from my mistakes.

Clarity about your personal mission creates clarity about the mission you're leading people into at work. When was the last time you revisited your organization's mission statement personally? When's the last time your team evaluated how closely aligned your work and priorities are to the team's purpose? Because if you clarify your personal mission and align your mission with the mission of the organization you serve, you'll reach your outcomes faster and with fewer distractions. That's what we learn from this fundamental principle of Jesus' leadership.

JESUS' MISSION STATEMENT

Jesus could have come to earth to overthrow the Roman government and reestablish the Jewish people into power. He could have spent all his time teaching how he fulfilled the Old Testament Scriptures. Or he could have chosen to stay in Jerusalem with the religious leaders connected to the Temple. Instead, Jesus had one simple focus: seeking and saving the lost.

Jesus' mission is my mission and your mission too—the mission of every person who follows him. But I want us to get more personal, to figure out what we can learn from his approach that will equip us to understand the specific missions he's given each of us. Let's notice together the way Jesus defined his mission:

- *who* he declared it to,
- *when* he decided to disclose it, and
- *what words* he used to describe the mission that changed all our lives.

Luke's Gospel highlights the many ways Jesus proved himself to be God, and it's obvious to anyone who spends time reading that Gospel that Luke organized the stories to help us all arrive at the same conclusion: Jesus was on a mission to seek and save the lost. Luke wrote as much in Luke 19:10, where Jesus speaks to a man named Zacchaeus.

Let's think about the *who* for a second. Zacchaeus was not a quality guy. He was a tax collector, and tax collectors were untrustworthy, greedy sellouts—or at least that was their stereotype. As my coauthor, Kat Armstrong, notes in her Bible study *Sinners*, tax collectors collected taxes for the Roman government. And since tax collectors earned their living by demanding more from the people being taxed than the Romans required, corruption was widespread in the industry. Many tax collectors overtaxed people to take their slice of the pie.[3]

The *when* is important to help us understand the context of what Jesus was saying about *who* he came to seek and save. During this moment in history, the Jews were suffering under Roman oppression. Roman taxes made life for the lower socioeconomic class unbearable—almost not survivable. The money the tax collectors extorted went into the silklined pockets of the Roman emperor as well as to the tax collectors themselves. To the Jews, tax collectors were robbers of what was due to God, so Jews equated tax collection with treason against God himself.

All that to say that in Jesus' time "tax collectors were hated, judged, and considered traitors."[4] That's why Jesus' conversation with Zacchaeus, a tax collector, is so surprising. Jesus initiated a conversation with one of the most hated men in Jericho during a time in history when Zacchaeus was a known enemy of God's people, participating in the corruption and harm caused by the oppressors. And Jesus purposed this moment in his ministry to make his mission statement public.

Now let's consider *what words* Jesus used to define his mission:

"The Son of Man came to seek and to save the lost."
LUKE 19:10

It doesn't get clearer than that, does it? I'm convinced Jesus intended the *who*, *when*, and *what* of this shocking conversation with Zacchaeus to show us not only what he was called to do but also how he was going to go about fulfilling his mission.

- **He was simple.** Many other people lived in Jericho, but Jesus sought out Zacchaeus. Because Jesus' mission was focused on seeking and saving the lost, he was focused on seeking and saving Zacchaeus. When Jesus said "lost," he meant the worst of the worst—even the despised. There's nothing complicated about it. It's so simple we might be tempted to miss the point altogether.

- **He was steadfast.** Jesus could have preached a long sermon or told a parable to illustrate his declaration, but instead he invited himself into Zacchaeus's home, defying Jewish tradition and disgusting everyone witnessing that moment in history. In short, Jesus was steadfast in his mission even when it sullied his reputation.

- **He was serious.** The last thing I want to point out here is that Jesus' conversation with Zacchaeus was serious. It had serious implications and changed the course of history. When Jesus said that he would be the one to seek out the lost and that he would be their Savior, he was also saying that Caesar, the Roman emperor, was not the Savior. That is part of what got Jesus killed. He challenged Caesar's power and authority. Jesus claimed, and then proved, that he was Lord of all and Caesar was not.

WHAT IS YOUR MISSION?

To live on mission like Jesus, we need to pursue our missions with simplicity, live our missions steadfastly, and take our missions seriously. But before we can do that, we need to be clear on what our personal missions are.

Why do I want you to start with your personal mission? Well, maybe you need to be reminded that you are indeed here on earth for a purpose. Yes, you. You were created by God and for God, to enjoy God. And your life on earth matters. *You* matter. You bear God's image. You reflect God's character. God has given you gifts to steward. And along the journey, the stewardship of those gifts will bring joy to your life and good to your community. Everyone benefits when you bring your gifts, talents, and treasures to the table and offer them to glorify God.

You're needed. The Kingdom is not the same without your contributions, and no one can replace you. You're one of a kind.

Usually, you're probably the one saying these things to the people you lead. But do you really believe these truths *for yourself*? Are you leading from a place of worthiness, wholeness, dignity, and value? Are you leading loved?

Let these familiar truths about your sacred identity in Christ and your invaluable presence in God's Kingdom resonate. Let them settle into your soul. Don't just gloss over them as if you've heard them all before.

Take a moment and appreciate the fact that you have purpose, that God's called you to do good works. He's done all the prep work for you to carry out your mission. You just have to walk in it.

So now let's get practical. I'm going to help you get started on a mission statement of your own.

1. As you seek God's guidance on your mission statement, answer these questions:

    - What are the unique gifts—the gifts that people around you recognize as special or uncommon—that God has given you?

    - What are the elite gifts—the gifts you excel in most or the gifts that set you apart from other leaders—that God has given you?

    - What adjectives do people use when they describe you?

- Is there a specific group of people for whom God has given you a tender heart?

- Are there things you love to do so much that you often volunteer to do them for free?

- Are there things you enjoy doing so much that you lose track of time when you do them?

Scan this QR code to download a guide with more questions I have used to help top leaders unearth the next level of their mission statement.

2. Considering your answers to those questions, what jumps out at you? What key words, phrases, verses, or stories come to mind? Make note of those things here:

Now you're ready to write out your mission statement.

To all the perfectionists: Don't fret. Your first draft will not be screen-printed on any T-shirts or blazoned across the landing page of your website. Write out your first draft and then revise, revise, revise. But you must start somewhere.

To all the visionary leaders: Don't assume you've already nailed this exercise and it's beneath you. Take some time to complete the following sentence but also to reevaluate whether that's really what you're on this earth to do in this season.

3. Finish this sentence using only eight words:

I exist to _____ _____ _____ _____

_____ _____ _____ _____.

I realize that exercises like this can impact us all differently. For some, reflecting on your purpose might be less tangible and granular than the tasks you spend most of your time doing at work. Purpose seems so elusive and ethereal, and it's uncomfortable to try to put it into words. You'd rather just get your tasks done and move on to the next list. That's okay.

Let your purpose lift you up from the daily grind. Allow this unusual task to encourage you.

Or maybe you're the kind of person who never stops thinking about this. You could rattle off your purpose statement because you've got it plastered on the walls in your office. You write it in your journals, or you've got an elevator pitch ready to share how God has purposed you. If that's you, I want to suggest that part of why you are doing this exercise is to clarify or adapt what you usually say to something more specific and relevant to this season of your leadership.

Now that you have a working personal mission statement, I want to give you a challenge:

- Have you communicated your mission statement to everyone who needs to hear it?
- Do the people you lead know why you're called to your organization and why your work matters to you on such a personal level?
- Can they identify why you're in the right role and how your personal mission statement aligns with the goals of your organization?

You and I spend most of our time as leaders addressing time-sensitive needs that cannot be overlooked. But today, let's step back and pause long enough to reflect on your mission statement. Personal and organizational mission statements shift a leader from living a powerless, reactive, and constantly-putting-out-fires style of leadership to living a potent, self-directed, and proactive one.

Maybe you are feeling unmotivated, defeated, overwhelmed,

and burned out. And maybe you feel that way because of things that have happened to you—factors that are, at least in part, beyond your control. But maybe you are feeling that way because you're working without your mission clarified. Could it be that part of what you're feeling is a lack of mission alignment? Because when your life is aligned with your purpose, when you know your purpose and live it, God's power carries you through inevitable challenges and causes you to stand your ground and carry on with determination.

MISSION-MINDED LEADERS ARE EASY TO FOLLOW

Unless you're deeply invested in the Bible translation industry, you've likely never heard the name Katharine Barnwell. Neither had I. But now I know: Katharine Barnwell is a spiritual giant.

Katharine was born in 1938. She was a trailblazer, attending St Andrews at a time when very few women attended university. It was there that George Cowan, the president of Wycliffe Bible Translators, shared with Katharine the great need for Bible translators. She commented, "That was it for me." She went on to translate the Bible for sixty years.[5]

That powerful, short phrase—*That was it for me*—communicates so much, doesn't it? Katharine knew what she was all about. She knew her mission in life. She became an innovative and devoted leader who changed the continent of Africa for Christ, catalyzed thousands of Bible translators around the world, and wrote the textbook for best practices on Bible translation. Katharine's purpose empowered her to transform the landscape of Bible translation methods, to accelerate the spread of the gospel in Africa, and to redefine the whole industry's goals.

Living on purpose generates a supernatural power to advance a mission. That's because part of knowing and loving God is experiencing his unique purpose for each of us.

So now that we've started defining our missions, what would it look like for us to follow Jesus' example and pursue our missions with simplicity, live our missions steadfastly, and take our missions seriously?

PURSUE YOUR MISSION WITH SIMPLICITY

Jesus had infinite options available to him to accomplish his mission of seeking and saving the lost, but he zeroed in on three things: teaching, preaching, and healing.

If you go through all four Gospels, you'll start to see a pattern. Everywhere Jesus went he was doing powerful things. But he didn't use one hundred different methods. He focused on three. He kept it simple, and I think we should too.

When I was on staff at a megachurch, attending leadership conferences was considered one of the most effective ways to grow as a Christian leader. I'd attend keynotes and breakouts to hear about ways leaders in other contexts were living out their purposes. They were smart people, strategic people who had developed tools and processes that equipped them to thrive in their communities and contexts of ministry. A lot of what they had to say encouraged me, and I felt challenged to take their ideas back to my teams.

But in retrospect, I was trying too hard to do too many things. I should have kept it simpler. I should have narrowed our focus and better defined our priorities.

Simply put, you need to simplify your life. And it will make you easier to follow.

It might not be preaching, teaching, and healing you need to focus on, but I know God has called you into something special, something only you can do for the Kingdom. What is it that you need to prioritize? What two or three things do you need to focus on to fulfill your mission in this season?

God is not impressed with busy; God is pleased with fruitful.

With the teams I lead, I don't want people to tell me how busy they are—I want to hear the outcomes they've created. The goal is not to live fast and furious. The goal is to live focused and fruitful. And we do that when our priorities are simpler.

This might mean you start with a list of ten things you feel are crucial to fulfill your mission but then decide to focus on three for the time being. Sometimes less is more. More of your time and energy around fewer initiatives will maximize your efforts to live into your calling.

Why don't you give that a try?

Crucial Priorities

1. _____

2. _____

3. _____

4. _____

5. _____

6. _____

7. _____

8. _____

9. _____

10. _____

Focused Goals

1. _____

2. _____

3. _____

Yes, doing this might mean you move at a slower pace. But you'll also make a deeper, stronger impact.

LIVE YOUR MISSION STEADFASTLY

I'm a world-class starter. In fact, we have a sign in our kitchen that says "Healthy eating starts tomorrow." But call me a day later and see how that's going. Some weeks I'm on fire and I make it three or four days before I end up in the Taco Bell drive-through or with a gallon of Blue Bell ice cream. Why? Because starting things is so much easier than finishing them.

Your issue may not be an eating plan, but I'd bet money you're as good at starting things as I am. Most leaders are great at the beginning. We start new initiatives, workout plans, diets, org charts, and budgets. We start relationships well. And sometimes we end them very, very poorly. But Jesus lived on mission steadfastly. He didn't start and stop his mission; his faithfulness carried on despite the challenges he faced.

That's why I believe any leader eager to lead like Jesus needs to live their mission steadfastly.

In our context, being *steadfast* means being unwavering about your personal and team missions, committed to your values even if it comes at a cost, and resilient when faced with adversity.

In Luke 2, we learn that Mary and Joseph brought Jesus to Jerusalem for Passover, and as they started to head home, they realized Jesus was missing. We might imagine they started asking each other, "Do you have Jesus?" Joseph would say, "I thought *you* had him." And Mary would say, "I thought *you* had him." (This is the *Home Alone* section of the Gospels.)

Mary and Joseph found Jesus all the way back at the Temple. And here's what Jesus said to his parents: "Didn't you know that I must be in Father's house?"[6] Remember, Jesus was a twelve-year-old boy at the time. It wasn't until more than twenty years later, on the cross at Calvary, that Jesus finally said, "It is finished."

He was all about his Father's business—about his mission to seek and save the lost—until the very end. Jesus persisted in his mission even when it cost him his life.

Not all of us are as steadfast as Jesus. I have invested most of my career in two primary vocations, education and ministry.

In both industries, the retention statistics are astoundingly low. In a recent Barna Group study, 38 percent of pastors surveyed indicated they were considering quitting full-time ministry.[7] Public educators reflect a similar pattern; over 50 percent of educators are considering leaving education before retirement.[8] Ministry is difficult. Teaching is hard, emotional, exhausting work. But those realities alone cannot account for these disappointing retention statistics. In 1 Corinthians 15:58, Paul encourages us to be "steadfast" and "immovable" in the work of the Lord (NRSV). The mission that God has invited you to is much more than a career; it is a calling—a calling that he will sustain you in as you remain surrendered to his will and steadfast in your mission.

TAKE YOUR MISSION SERIOUSLY

Nothing could get in the way of Jesus fulfilling his mission. Yes, part of the reason nothing thwarted his plan was because he's the Lord of lords and the King of the universe. But the intentionality, perseverance, and commitment he had toward his mission can and should direct us as leaders. If Jesus took his mission seriously, so should we.

There's one Bible story where Jesus always catches me off guard in his commitment to his mission. In Matthew 12, Jesus becomes aware that his mother and brothers are nearby waiting to talk to him. Instead of Jesus responding the way we might assume, with something like "Send them in" or "I can't wait to see them" or "Good! I love my family," he uses the moment to clarify just how serious he is about his mission. Jesus asks, "Who is my mother, and who are my brothers?"[9] And then he motions toward his disciples and identifies them as his real family. His point? Jesus' mission to seek and save the lost changed how he defined family.

Jesus was in no way disrespecting his mother or his other family members; we know that Jesus ensured the care of his family while he was on the cross, asking John to watch over his mother in his absence. When Jesus says that his disciples are his family, he is declaring that he takes his mission so seriously that *it redefines who he is closest to*.

Your mission will redefine your priorities, and it should. Your mission might confuse the people around you. Your mission could even cause rifts in your family. But if your mission is God given, if you're willing to simplify your life to pursue your mission steadfastly, you have to get serious about it.

As a pastor I have had the privilege of being with many people at the ends of their lives. When I care for someone who knows their days are limited, they will often share their joys and their regrets. At the end of a life, the greatest regrets are often the chances a person didn't take or the opportunities they didn't embrace with sufficient urgency. They wish they had been more serious about what God had placed before them.

Let's make a covenant together today that we will be leaders who understand and have lived these great words from Theodore Roosevelt:

> It is not the critic who counts; not the man who points out how the strong man stumbles, or where the doer of deeds could have done them better. The credit belongs to the man who is actually in the arena, whose face is marred by dust and sweat and blood; who strives valiantly; who errs, who comes short again

and again, because there is no effort without error and shortcoming; but who does actually strive to do the deeds; who knows the great enthusiasms, the great devotions; who spends himself in a worthy cause; who at the best knows in the end the triumph of high achievement, and who at the worst, if he fails, at least fails while daring greatly, so that his place shall never be with those cold and timid souls who neither know victory nor defeat.[10]

PERSONAL REFLECTION QUESTIONS

Write out your answers before you go to bed tonight.

1. **Clarify your mission statement:** What's the one thing I'm here to do? What spurs me on and gets my heart racing? What do I want said about me at my eightieth birthday party?

2. **Pursue your mission with simplicity:** What is it that I need to prioritize? What two or three things do I need to focus on to fulfill my mission in this season?

3. **Live your mission steadfastly:** In the past, what has hindered the pursuit of my mission? What causes my hope to waver? Am I impacted by fear or by focusing too much on past mistakes or hurts?

4. **Take your mission seriously:** A personal mission is never only personal. If I fulfill my mission, who benefits? If I don't fulfill my mission, what's the cost to the people I serve?

TEAM DISCUSSION QUESTIONS

Ask these questions during your next team meeting.

1. Is the mission statement for our team or organization as clear as it needs to be?
2. Who in our organization needs to be reminded of our mission statement?
3. Have we done everything possible to align our resources (time, money, and people) with the mission of our organization?

INVITATIONAL QUESTIONS FOR FEEDBACK

Using one of these questions, ask at least one person you lead for feedback in the next seven days.

1. What would you say is your personal mission statement? In other words, what would you say is the reason you are here on earth? What is the reason you are in this role?
2. How have I helped or hindered your pursuit of your defined mission?
3. When I share my personal mission statement with you, are you surprised? Or do my daily actions, passions, and priorities reflect the mission I declare?

THREE

JESUS TAUGHT HIS METHODS; HE DIDN'T JUST TELL THEM

One day as he saw the crowds gathering, Jesus went up on the mountainside and sat down. His disciples gathered around him, and he began to teach them.
MATTHEW 5:1-2, NLT

One of my great joys is consulting with and serving leadership teams at schools. As a former teacher and administrator, I'm delighted to get to spend a day on campus with no restrictions, encouraged to be a visitor to any classroom, practice, or meeting.

The school I was at on this particular day was a very good one, with a legacy of strong academics and robust extracurricular programs. With the reputation of the school in mind, I anticipated a high degree of consistency in what I would witness that day—that classroom cultures and student engagement levels would be similar across the campus. I was wrong.

As I walked down each hallway, I noticed a stark contrast. Some classes were high energy, with students and teachers interacting in a robust but respectful way. In one class, one of the oldest teachers in the school intentionally engaged students through social media. Other classes, though, had a more tepid vibe, with teachers dominating the conversations and students all resigned to a "sit and get" experience. Some classrooms were infected with the malaise that comes from the boredom of being told information with no attempt to make the delivery relevant, meaningful, or fun.

After witnessing this numerous times, I started trying to define what was different between the leadership styles of the teachers. After stopping in a couple more stops in classrooms, it became very clear. In the high-energy classes, the teachers were actually teaching, but in the other classroom environments, the teachers were telling the students how to behave, what to do, and what to take away from the day's lesson rather than encouraging them to take ownership of their own learning and behavior.

The words *teaching* and *telling* sound very similar, but when you witness the contrast, you can't help but notice the incongruity.

Leaders who communicate primarily through telling are more focused on their personal agenda of doing their job without being mindful of the needs, expectations, or success of others. Tellers see communication as primarily a "give" proposition—they are giving information.

Teaching, on the other hand, is student focused: The teacher is engaged in teaching the students, not the subject matter. The lesson gets conveyed, but the teacher does so through a combination of lecture, questions and answers, unique activities relevant to the subject matter, and significant affirmation. A leader who teaches believes that they have a great treasure to share, a lesson that can propel the student to a new level of understanding and empowerment. Teachers see communication as more of a "give and receive" endeavor, striving to convey information that can be heard, understood, and acted upon.

There are essentially only two ways that a human being experiences learning. One is through experience. Experience is a hard path to learning. When we learn through experience, there is likely a cost—whether it's time, money, pain, or even relationships.

The other way we learn is through teaching. Teaching occurs when the experience of one benefits another person or group. Teaching involves sharing more than just basic information; teaching includes context that explains why that information matters. Telling rarely, if ever, facilitates learning.

What is your primary communication style? Are you a teller? Or are you a leader who takes seriously the knowledge and experiences you have and stewards them well as a teacher?

GREAT TEACHERS

What if, five years into the future, your team follows you not just because you are a leader but also because your investment in their lives has catalyzed their success? Your team huddles are enjoyable and efficient, an authentic reflection of your team cohesion, mission alignment, and noticeable organizational growth. Your team conquers every challenge thrown their way, and you're outperforming your highest expectations of the organization. All cylinders are firing with the horsepower of a Ferrari engine.

The leadership you're dreaming of will not be the result of *telling* your team what to do but rather *showing* them how to do it.

The difference between telling and teaching shows up in how people talk about your leadership. Do you suspect your team is saying things like "She talks a lot in meetings," "He sends long emails with directions and instructions," "My leader gets frustrated easily," or "When will I ever have clarity?" Or does your team say, "You taught us well"?

As an educator myself, I have had the joy and privilege of witnessing some amazing teachers. Some of them have been fun and kind; others strict and regimented. Their approach hasn't been what has set their teaching apart. They've been elite because their priority is student learning, not just presentation of lessons. The sign of good teaching is student comprehension.

The very best teachers stand out for three distinct reasons.

1. **Great teachers explain the why behind the lessons.** Students understand the context, the reason the information will be useful in the long run, and how the lesson fits into the rest of the class. At their core, the people you lead are all just grown-up kids asking the same question: *Why?* And if we fail to give reasonable answers, we won't be easy to follow in the classroom, boardroom, or church building. I've learned this vital truth: People are drawn to clarity. If I can't provide it, then I will never experience their full engagement.

2. **Great teachers model the desired outcomes of the teaching.** Students thrive when the teacher can model the skills that are the object of the lessons. Every student benefits from a coach who can demonstrate the techniques on the

field, a music teacher who can produce a quality sound from an instrument, or a math teacher who can solve a complex equation in real time in front of a class.

3. **Great teachers know that the goal of teaching is all about relationships.** What influences students most is not how much the teacher knows about the content but how much the teacher cares about them. The same is true for the people you lead. Yes, of course, they need you to be competent in your work. That's a given. But what your followers need most from you is not to understand how much you know but to experience how much you care. People are galvanized by a leader's empathy.

The reason teaching differs from telling is that teaching involves knowing an individual's needs, being intentional to meet those needs, and caring about who they are becoming—not just what they produce. In a team environment, the sense of connectedness that teaching produces between colleagues and managers increases communication, innovation, and job satisfaction, which ultimately leads to improved performance. Relational capital, the result of your affection, appreciation, and empathy for others, is your most valuable asset as a leader.[1]

Easy-to-follow leaders are great teachers, and Christ was chief among them. Jesus knew how to get his students—his disciples—to understand his lessons. He didn't bark orders at his followers or preach a bunch of long sermons or dictate instructions for godly living. He taught his messages through life-on-life learning opportunities where his followers could truly understand the meaning of becoming Christlike.

TEACH LIKE JESUS

If you're leading and feeling as if you don't have the resources or tools to lead well, I want to challenge you to read your Bible looking for three things:

1. the way Jesus introduced or followed up his instructions with parables,
2. the way Jesus referenced Old Testament stories as examples, and
3. the way Jesus included the disciples when he was interacting with people.

Jesus' example reveals this truth: Important lessons are not rules to be announced but methods to be practiced. Jesus told his disciples to turn the other cheek, care for the poor, and let their light shine before others,[2] but he also showed them what this looked like through his own ministry. He could have left us with instructions to resist retaliation when someone attacks us, but instead he went to the Cross in the ultimate act of nonretaliation. Jesus could have sent word to his followers to share their resources with the economically disadvantaged, but instead he flipped over tables in the Temple when the worship of God excluded the poorest in Jerusalem.[3] And Jesus could have recommended being a bright witness for Christ through our actions and words, but instead he modeled this for us as the Light of the World.[4]

When Jesus wanted to get a message across to his disciples, he modeled the lesson.

Think about it—all growth requires teaching and intentional

modeling. We don't let just anyone perform brain surgery. No. We require brain surgeons to go to medical school, take an enormous number of tests, and then put in hundreds of hours of practice under the careful supervision of proven leaders. Your parents didn't throw you the keys to a brand-new luxury vehicle the day you turned sixteen. They put you in driver's education first, and they spent countless terrifying hours riding shotgun while you learned to merge onto an interstate and parallel park. All the essential things we do every day as people were not just communicated to us but learned through witnessing the proper way to do it, practicing (a lot), and being given the opportunity to fail and try again.

Why would leadership be any different? If there are crucial aspects of your organization that you want to saturate your teams, don't depend on a poster in the break room or a sentence on your website to define your culture. If you have essential behaviors everyone in your organization needs to live out, guess what? It's your job to model the behaviors with unyielding consistency and commitment. *You* set the tone. *You* are the example. An organization's culture is defined by the behaviors its leaders teach, tolerate, celebrate, and model.

Jesus could have carved the Great Commandment onto stone tablets, but he chose to write it on our hearts through his embodied presence on earth. He didn't just want us to read about his methods; he needed his disciples to experience them. Jesus could have spoken to his disciples from heaven, shouting down to earth with a cosmic megaphone to announce the importance of loving God and loving others—but instead he chose to wait until someone asked a question and answered it in real time so that his disciples could hear his voice and stand eye to eye in a conversation they'd never forget.

Christ did not avoid the truth or resist declaring his instructions. But he also didn't leave it at that. He went the extra mile—or miles from heaven—to come down to earth and be with his people to teach. Is there any one of his followers who would question his motives? No. Any one of his disciples who would speculate about his devoted care for them, not just as a group but also as individuals? Again, no.

Jesus was easy to follow because everyone knew he cared about the people he was committed to teaching and he was intentional to explain the why behind his lessons.

If you want to become an easy-to-follow leader, become an exceptional teacher who facilitates trusting relationships. Most leaders can command respect, but earning it through trusted relationships is the way of Christ. Need your people to listen harder, catch on quicker, and "get it"? Deepen your relationships, be more present, ask better questions, listen twice as much, offer answers generously, and be patient.

When Jesus led the disciples to Caesarea Philippi, he demonstrated this technique by first gathering his disciples in a small group and asking a general question: "Who do people say the Son of Man is?" He then asked a more specific question: "Who do you say I am?"[5] And then he patiently started the process of explaining to them that he would be handed over, tortured, and crucified.

My daughter, Jordie, is a passionate Christ follower, so she began her career as an elementary teacher committed to teaching like Jesus. She was deeply invested in all her students, but the kids with learning differences and those living through hard circumstances held a special place in her tender heart. One such student—we will call him Trevor—meant a lot to Jordie. She worked overtime to win his trust and show she cared about him in and outside of the classroom.

One day, a fellow teacher approached her and asked if Trevor could come to Jordie's class to do his schoolwork for a different subject. You see, Trevor found that just being near Jordie increased his ability to get his work done. Jordie created a safe, loving environment where all her kids thrived, but for Trevor that environment was a safe harbor in a stormy, wave-crashing life. Trevor's other teachers knew that if he needed to really concentrate, he needed to sit in Jordie's classroom.

Doesn't that sound a lot like Jesus? He's our safe harbor as leaders. He's the one who provides calm to our storms.

If you desire more influence as a leader, start working on relational equity earned through teaching. Anyone with credibility can tell people what to do. But to have influence, you need to learn how to teach. Of course Jesus is a credible leader. He is the Son of God; his deity is his business-card title. But Jesus shows us that effective teams need leaders who are not only credible but also influential—leaders who speak with authority and are respected by their people.

I know this shift in your focus could be a little intimidating. Especially for leaders with a lot of practice telling and less practice teaching.

Remember—when Jesus commissioned his disciples, he entrusted them to do the work he'd prepared them to do in the three years of his earthly ministry. For the first time in their leadership journey, the disciples were charged with all God's authority to change the world by teaching everything Christ had taught them. To pass on the lessons learned. Jesus knew that the great commission was an impossible task—unless, of course, they had his abiding presence. How did Jesus ready his leaders to carry on his Kingdom work? He told them, "I am with you always."[6]

Don't miss the message of this chapter. Teaching is relationship. Teaching stands next to you. Teaching is *with*. And your great teacher, Jesus, is with you now and always. You're not leading alone.

Leaders who tell . . .
- give monologues;
- shame others for having to repeat themselves;
- have underperforming team members;
- blame those who "don't get it";
- bark things like "you have to," "you should," and "you need to"; and
- get irritated when their preferences are not prioritized.

Leaders who teach . . .
- ask and answer lots of questions;
- invite students into conversations;
- share relevant stories;
- use illustrations to make their points;
- make the lessons about their students, not the teacher; and
- take time to explain their rationale.

With relationship as the priority, easy-to-follow leaders create . . .

- **Safety.** Leaders who create shame-free zones and learning opportunities do so by cultivating environments where learners know they will not be chastised or threatened or experience consequences for trying new things, asking hard questions, or needing more clarity. These leaders often focus on getting "better" rather than quantifying results as either "good" or "bad."

- **Security.** Many leaders resist innovation, calculated risks, and thinking outside the box because somewhere along the way in their leadership journeys they were scared or hurt. Leader, make sure your learners know that they are safe to make mistakes and that you'll be there to support them no matter what.

- **Success.** Nobody wants to be average. Growing leaders want to experience success and multiply success in others. That's why easy-to-follow leaders create wins for their teams. They set them up for success, not failure. They don't test their knowledge to catch them in pitfalls; they ready others to reach their desired outcomes.

Leader, if you strive to be a great teacher—answering the *why*, modeling the outcomes, and showing your people how much you care by creating safety, security, and success—the truths you want them to understand will be seeds of knowledge that sprout and grow into fruitful trees. Your team members will flourish, and their flourishing will benefit the whole organization—you included.

YOU CAN CHANGE

I'm a recovering telling leader, and I've served telling leaders too. Whether I've been on the giving or receiving end of this kind of leadership, it hasn't been any fun for anybody. I look back at my time in toxic organizations with gratitude that God has redeemed my time in them and carried me through what felt like an insufferable number of trials, but I also carry with me some regrets—the kind of regrets that form you as a leader.

Here's what I've learned about being a telling leader: You can change.

You don't have to carry on impatiently or with an uncaring attitude. God can give you a hunger to support your team with a mastery level of teaching skills, and the Holy Spirit can accompany you in every effort you make to create a culture of avid learners.

When I look back at my time as a leader who chose to tell rather than teach, I see some telltale signs that the leaders around me were not getting my best. These signs are likely present in leaders who tell instead of teach. You might be a telling leader if this is your experience:

1. Your team struggles to understand why you do the things you are doing.

2. Your team doesn't have well-defined wins or measurements of success.

3. You tell your team to "get this done" without giving them an opportunity to ask for clarity.

4. You assume that if things are easy and obvious to you, then other people should similarly have no problems.
5. You feel the need to closely monitor your team's tasks and productivity.
6. You've given your team permission to act, but they still struggle to accomplish your goals.

Leader, you have two choices: explain or explode. If you keep telling and not teaching, eventually you are going to explode in anger or frustration. That's why the extremes of telling leaders have had a lasting impact on the leaders God has called me to shepherd. If you long to become a teacher instead, I want to challenge you to accept God's grace in your leadership. Repent for your bad behavior, make amends where needed, and receive God's forgiveness so that you can grow into a teaching leader. Then start explaining your decisions and teach others to do the same. To do so, you'll need to change some of your practices, and you will certainly need to change your pace. Teaching takes time, but in the end the investment is always well worth it.

I know of one college basketball coach who came to the revelation that he had been a telling leader for much of his career. To own his failures and make amends, he sent a personal letter of apology to every player who had played under his leadership for the past twenty-plus years. Humility like this creates a hunger to lead differently in the future.

The way of Jesus is to empower leaders. He deputized the disciples with his authority and power to carry forth his presence and practice the lessons he'd so effectively taught those he loved. Jesus was patient and caring. He welcomed questions and gave meaningful answers without making anyone feel stupid. And he kept his disciples mission focused on the highest priorities of the Father.

Abandon telling for teaching. Jesus will show you the way, and your leadership will change for the better.

PERSONAL REFLECTION QUESTIONS
Write out your answers before you go to bed tonight.

1. Am I more focused on developing the people around me or driving results that feed my ego and identity?

2. Which of the three signs of great teaching—safety, security, success—am I executing well? Which need some improvement?

3. Can I name at least three people who have grown significantly under my leadership in the past five years?

4. How often do I react in frustration and criticism when I could be teaching and encouraging? How can I intentionally pause in those moments to start choosing a different response?

TEAM DISCUSSION QUESTIONS

Ask these questions during your next team meeting.

1. When have you felt led well by me?
2. What do I do that makes your job easier? Harder?
3. Do you have all the clarity you need from me?

INVITATIONAL QUESTIONS FOR FEEDBACK

Using one of these questions, ask at least one person you lead for feedback in the next seven days.

1. Have I been a leader who has accelerated your growth, or have I hindered it? How can I be more effective in the future?
2. Have I taught and trained you in the skills you need to be successful in your role? Are there any skills you are lacking?
3. Have I clearly defined the *why* behind what you are being asked to do as well as the *win* in doing it?

FOUR

JESUS MENTORED, NOT MANAGED, HIS TEAM

"Students are not greater than their teacher. But the student who is fully trained will become like the teacher."
JESUS (LUKE 6:40, NLT)

Very early in my consulting career I had an incredible mentor. He was intelligent, was personable, and had an immense amount of wisdom. He was assigned to oversee my onboarding and development in my new role, and in our first few meetings I was struck by how much I talked and how well he listened. He just kept asking questions. He asked me straightforward questions about my background, my goals, and my relevant experiences as well as complex questions about how I would handle certain types of people and situations.

I was with the company just a couple of weeks when he and I got an opportunity to go to Atlanta to serve a national communications company. The assignment was simple: We would work with one of their teams for two days, and if that team was impressed with our tools and processes, we would be given a significant opportunity to serve teams throughout that region.

My mentor and I had a plan going into the engagement, and we partnered throughout the first day. But on the morning of the second day, my mentor told me that he had been impressed with me and that he was confident I could serve the team by myself that day. He said he had a couple of other people to meet with while we were in town and wished me well as I engaged with the group—my first solo day as a corporate consultant.

The second day didn't go well. They asked me some questions that I wasn't totally prepared to handle; I didn't teach some of our principles with clarity and conviction; and I didn't manage the flow and timing of the day effectively.

When I got back to the hotel, my mentor was waiting for me. I told him it had been a disaster and that the renewal was very, very unlikely. He smiled and asked me to go up to my room and list all the things I would do differently if I had a second chance. Two hours later I met him for dinner, and we talked through the list. He was kind but direct as he coached me through the areas I felt were subpar. As we were finishing, I apologized again and said, "I know the next contract was going be worth $50,000. I am so sorry I cost you that money." My mentor smiled and replied, "You learned many valuable lessons today. I'll call that lost money tuition, because you are going to produce millions of dollars for this company."

I have maintained a lifelong relationship with this mentor. I did end up leading some of the largest engagements in their company history, and I worked with him for over twenty years. It may not surprise you that my mentor's company has an employee retention rate of nearly 90 percent.

About the same time that I started my consulting career, a very good friend of mine made the transition from corporate work to ministry. He had been offered a role at one of the nation's largest churches and would be working directly with the senior pastor. My friend was very excited to lean into his new role and learn from his pastor. We talked often, and we were both surprised at how different our onboarding journeys were. My friend went to meetings with his pastor but was never asked a question. He was told to take notes, mandated to do things in a very specific way, and often instructed to write direct quotes that he was to use in talking to other members of the staff. My friend shared with me that he wasn't even certain of the expectations for his role. He had no level of empowerment, was given only menial tasks, and had no rhythm of communication with his leader. After feeling immense frustration and being told he was failing multiple times, he left his role in under twelve months.

My friend had come into his new role hoping and expecting to experience a similar level of mentoring and leadership that I did. However, he instead learned a valuable lesson about how it feels to be managed, to be treated as simply an asset in an organization rather than as a valuable human being with resources to offer. He wasn't the only young leader who had a short tenure there; many other gifted leaders who were seen as disappointments left that church only to experience significance and success at other ministries.

The biggest takeaway from these two examples is simply this: A manager is only concerned about today when it comes to employee performance and productivity; mentors are focused on tomorrow. A mentor looks to provide lessons and leadership that will create a successful tomorrow for their people.

ASSETS OR PEOPLE?

When I started talking with a retired army commander in his second career as a church leader, he told me about the whiplash. He left an organization that was, in his words, solely focused on mentorship and leadership, and he expected to encounter the same intentionality in church work. Instead, he described "leaving something all about leadership to join church staff and focus entirely on management."

A retired executive pastor confided in me that after his church's most expansive season of growth, many of his most capable leaders quit. Their reason? They'd been overmanaged as the church had grown. Before the congregation size increased, the church leaders primarily focused on developing and building into the church staff. But as soon as attendance grew, the focus shifted from growing leaders to managing all the new members.

As a leader, you probably think a lot in terms of management. Management is about resources—the tangible and intangible assets of your organization that help you reach your outcomes. Management is all about directing the assets to reach certain outcomes, and the goal of management is compliance.

Management plays a vital role in every organization, but a leader who focuses solely on managing their human resources *talks at* those they lead but never *listens to* them. They *assign* delegated tasks but never *empower* their team to do meaningful work. People learn what to expect but are never taught how to respond.

So what's the solution?

Leader, I want to challenge you to think about how you can become more intentional about developing a *mentorship* mentality to coincide with the practices of management. Whether you're in an executive role in your organization, in middle management, or a mentee without any direct reports, growing as a leader means shifting your focus from managing others (or being managed by others) to mentoring others and being mentored by others.

Management and mentorship are not the same thing. Based on Jesus' example, mentoring positions us and those we lead for long-term impact, because instead of focusing on resources, we prioritize the needs of people.

THE JESUS APPROACH

In chapter 10 of Matthew's Gospel, we see Jesus preparing his disciples for their first missionary journey. Then, a few chapters later, Jesus pulls his disciples aside and tells them, "If any want to become my followers, let them deny themselves and take up their cross and follow me."[1] At first glance, these may not seem like clear mentoring moments, but Jesus, both in how he prepared the disciples and in what he communicated, shows us seven key approaches of a mentor.

Matthew 10: Jesus sends out the disciples to do ministry on their own.

1. **Demonstrating the behaviors he wanted them to emulate.** Before Jesus commissioned his disciples to do as he had done, he showed them how to do it. Ahead of the commissioning in Matthew 10, Jesus finished several

miraculous healings and completed several encounters with people who needed the gospel news. Only after he'd shown the disciples the way did he summon them and give them authority to heal and preach in his name.

2. **Giving clear instructions and authority.** Great mentors know how to set realistic expectations to prepare their followers for inevitable challenges. Jesus' directions to the disciples were clear: Go to the lost sheep of Israel, proclaim the good news that the Kingdom of Heaven has come near, cure the sick, raise the dead, and cast out demons.[2] Basically *Do everything you've seen me do on our journeys together.* Jesus even prepared his disciples for how to survive persecution.

3. **Offering opportunities to practice.** This first missionary journey was a practice mission, giving the disciples opportunities to do things they'd never done before. Jesus is a wise leader. He knew the people following him and watching him needed to move beyond managing the responses of newly healed people into facilitating ministry themselves. That new phase of ministry would require Jesus' mentorship.

4. **Setting the standard for a job well done.** Christ didn't kick up his feet and take a vacation after sending out his team to multiply his healing and gospel-proclaiming efforts. No—as Matthew 11:1 says, "When Jesus had finished instructing his twelve disciples, he went on from there to teach and proclaim his message in their cities" (NRSV). Jesus didn't stop mentoring; he continued setting

the standard for a job well done. Implicit in this section of Scripture is that Jesus was doing this work alongside his disciples. He prepared them, but he also practiced with them.

Matthew 16: Jesus tells his disciples about his coming suffering, death, and resurrection.

5. **Explaining what to anticipate.** Jesus' words about *taking up their cross* (Matthew 16:24) must have terrified the men and women devoted to following him. But here's what his approach teaches us about mentoring well: Jesus took the time to explain what his leaders were going to experience in the future rather than expecting them to think on their feet or "pay their dues" when blindsided by challenges.

   Leader, we need to do the same if we want to be easy to follow. We can't just throw our teams to the wolves or create scenarios they are unprepared for. Instead, leadership is about walking others through the potential pitfalls of their role and strengthening their confidence through preparation.

6. **Offering an invitation to follow him.** Next, Jesus extended an invitation to his followers to make a crucial exchange, trading the life they had known for the promise and rewards of heaven. Accepting this invitation to follow would come with a cost. As leaders it is important that we clarify for others the cost of their desired path and the consequences of choosing that path. As a coach, I never had a player who didn't say they wanted to

be great. It was my role as their leader to communicate the cost of developing their talents to that level and the consequences of that choice. I do the same as a business leader when I hire and as a pastor when I counsel young couples prior to their marriages.

7. **Going first.** Despite the high cost, many of those disciples accepted Jesus' invitation to forfeit their lives to enjoy eternal life with Christ. Why? Because Jesus went first.

Part of the reason our trust in leaders is eroding is because we have a generation of leaders too tired or maybe unwilling to be the first to fulfill the mandates we set for our teams. Leaders who won't go first will end up with teams who finish last. That's why going first is one of the most fundamental aspects of easy-to-follow leaders. They don't push their leaders to the edge of a diving board and scream, "Jump!" Just the opposite. Easy-to-follow leaders mentor their leaders to the edge of the deep end of any leadership pool with the encouragement "I wouldn't ask you to face any challenge I haven't already faced."

MENTORING TO MULTIPLY

Leadership, in all its forms, can feel like you are on an island. That's why what we need most as leaders is not to be managed but to be mentored. Yes, management is a key aspect of any organizational structure—every organization needs someone to be the ultimate point of responsibility and accountability. But every single leader on your team and in your life needs a mentor, too (including you). A mentor is someone to discuss new ideas with, someone to teach you the ropes. And a mentor's leadership impact continues long after they're gone.

When I entered my first year as a science schoolteacher at a suburban Denver public school, the various districts gathered several hundred new teachers for training. I soon discovered that our trainers were former teachers, most of whom had been out of the classroom for many years. And they were going to talk—not *with* us, but *at* us—for hours. We incoming teachers also took a test that provided us with a multitude of data points, but no one took the time to explain what the results meant about me or my role as a teacher.

I realize that a lot has changed in school systems since I was an educator, but back then, I walked into my first classroom, on my first day, blind. I didn't have a single tool in my teaching tool belt to do my job well. And I concluded that if I needed to be mentored as a new teacher, my training was not going to cut it. That's why God sent me Rick.

Rick's classroom was right next to mine, and I studied his teaching style, looking for ways to learn the ropes of running a classroom. I watched carefully as he'd set up his lessons, combining a variety of activities to reach the varied learning styles of his students. And I watched Rick build rapport with the students in his classroom. He mastered the art of connecting with the students, learning what motivated them, taking a vested interest in their lives outside of school.

Rick's example taught me more than any training could have. He was my real-world, real-time example of a teacher making a difference in the lives of his students. Eventually I shifted from being an intentional observer of Rick's methods to asking questions out of curiosity. I started asking Rick all my teacher questions, and over time he unofficially became my mentor.

I must have asked Rick questions for months, and each day he was patient, caring, and funny, and best of all, he knew how to downplay my roughest days as a new teacher. Rick knew how to encourage me but also how to push me into growth. He could tell it to me straight, but I always knew he meant his feedback in love. His goal was my success.

Isolation coupled with being a new leader who's underprepared could have been my pathway to burnout as a new teacher, but I stayed in the classroom as long as I did because of Rick. He was the ideal mentor, one who could effectively balance providing critical feedback with the nurture and encouragement that I needed to invest in the lives of young leaders for years to come.

That same year I began coaching at a high school in the district. The head coach who hired me took me to breakfast and *listened* to my heart as I explained why I wanted to become a coach. He provided me with mentors and experiences that *empowered* me to grow in my knowledge and coaching techniques. He allowed me to be part of every varsity practice so I could see experienced coaches *model* what effective coaching is and the impact it has on student-athletes.

If I'd only experienced management in that season, I likely would have felt the frustrations and failures that other young leaders have when they are left isolated and inexperienced by leaders who failed to pick up the mantle of being a mentor. My career in education would have been short and my impact on others very shallow. Instead, thanks to these mentors, and many others along the way, I invested more than two decades of my career in education, impacting thousands and multiplying my passion for teaching into dozens of my students who have gone on to become successful teachers and coaches. Mentorship is about helping others grow to their highest potential, even if that means growing their role beyond your team. The goal of mentorship is multiplication—launching the leaders around you to extend your impact and theirs.

Mentorship Mindset	Management Mindset
uses their life experiences to make the lives of team members easier	uses team members to make their own life easier
is determined to delegate and entrust	is tempted to micromanage
considers it a success when leaders outgrow the organization	wants leaders to stay at the organization
plants leaders in gardens, where they can flourish	puts leaders in pots to limit their growth at a given time
produces leaders who are highly engaged and empowered to take ownership	produces leaders who are less engaged with less ownership
goal: multiplication	*goal:* resource allocation

Jesus was focused on mentorship because he knew that the gospel could only advance through multiplication—first by Jesus multiplying into the disciples and then by those disciples multiplying into others. A pandemic can infect millions in a short period of time because the infection of one person can be quickly multiplied when shared with others. The love and lessons we have received from Christ can also multiply exponentially if we are leaders who are committed to living and leading with a mentorship mentality.

PERSONAL REFLECTION QUESTIONS

Write out your answers before you go to bed tonight.

1. When have I grown the most as a leader? Who was mentoring me in that season?

2. Under whose leadership have I grown the most and why?

3. Are the leaders serving with me growing? If I took an annual inventory, would I be able to see their growth over time? If I leave my role tomorrow, is there someone ready to take on my role?

TEAM DISCUSSION QUESTIONS

Ask these questions during your next team meeting.

1. When have you felt frustrated or overwhelmed by leadership?
2. What skills have I underdeveloped in you?
3. What additional resources, tools, or training do you need from me?

INVITATIONAL QUESTIONS FOR FEEDBACK

Using one of these questions, ask at least one person you lead for feedback in the next seven days.

1. Have I been a willing participant in your success—do you feel that I am available for, invested in, and excited about your growth as a leader?
2. Do you feel permitted to take risks and make mistakes?
3. Since you started working here, have you moved closer to your dreams and goals or further away from them?

FIVE

JESUS PRACTICED UNCOMMON COMPASSION

Jesus saw the huge crowd as he stepped from the boat, and he had compassion on them because they were like sheep without a shepherd. So he began teaching them many things.
MARK 6:34, NLT

Years ago, I met a man in Ethiopia who has since become a good friend. We share a love of sports, ministry, and greasy burgers. I met him when I was on a mission trip to Africa, and one day at lunch, he commented that he wished his country had a McDonald's. As I probed him with questions, he shared a fascinating story.

A few years before, a young nephew of my friend was diagnosed with a rare but treatable form of cancer. The challenge was that the hospital and doctors who specialize in treatment of this cancer were in Los Angeles. Through a ministry outreach, arrangements were made for the twelve-year-old boy to come to the United States to receive treatment, and due to some unique visa laws in Ethiopia, my friend was to accompany him, not his parents.

My friend and his nephew arrived in California for two months of treatment. Because my friend had very little money, he stayed the nights in the same hospital room as the boy. In fact, the only time he would leave the room was to go to the lobby each morning while the room was being cleaned. He would spend about an hour watching television there.

This is where the story gets interesting. One morning as my friend was watching TV, a woman approached him and greeted him warmly. She was a board member at the hospital and was waiting for some other members to arrive. As she waited, she was briefing herself on the agenda for an upcoming meeting, and evidently the television volume was proving distracting. She asked my friend if he would reduce the volume slightly. As they talked, she noticed his unique accent and inquired where he was from and why he was in Los Angeles. As my friend told her about his nephew, the woman became more and more interested in their circumstances.

The two finished the conversation, and the woman went to meet up with the other board members. That afternoon she returned to the hospital with her husband—an actor whose office contained multiple Oscars and Golden Globes and a Tony. They came to the nephew's room with gifts, treats, and a video game setup to keep the twelve-year-old entertained during his lengthy hospital stay. They also had a gift for my friend: They told him that he would be staying at their guesthouse and that a driver would take him back and forth to the hospital whenever he wanted.

That evening, after the boy had gone to sleep, the woman's

husband and the driver returned to the hospital to pick up my friend. On the way home the actor asked my friend if he was hungry, and they went through the McDonald's drive-through. My friend experienced his first Quarter Pounder with cheese that night, and a trip through the McDonald's drive-through became a nightly routine until my friend and his (completely healthy) nephew returned to Ethiopia months later.

I cannot imagine a better example of a person who could have, maybe even justifiably, been indifferent and yet chose compassion. The actor's wife was at the hospital to work, and she embraced a disruption in her day as an opportunity to meet someone new, engage in their story, and create a life-enhancing scenario for my friend and his sick nephew.

I know that most of us don't have the resources of a guesthouse or a chauffeur, but we all have something to offer others—our time, our prayers, *some resource*. Are you living a life of compassion, or have you let the responsibilities and distractions of the day make you indifferent to the circumstances and needs of others?

COMPASSIONATE LEADERSHIP

The longer I'm in leadership, the more convinced I become that we overvalue bravado, strong personality types, and brute force—and we undervalue faithfulness, empathy, and action-oriented love. Our whole evaluation system for leadership success is often skewed to reward the person who speaks the loudest or strikes the most fear into others. Our culture tends to praise and promote leaders with lots of aggression. But the Bible sets forth a radically different way of accomplishing goals, fulfilling mandates, and staying on mission.

When we look at Jesus, we see a man whose uncommon compassion—for the lonely, least, and lost—attracted, retained, and catalyzed an unlikely group of people to carry on his mission long after his ascension. Jesus went out of his way to love, support, and heal the types of people most leaders would deem unworthy of their attention. Some leadership books focus on finding the right people to support your vision, and while that can be helpful, Jesus modeled a subversive and controversial way of engaging with people who'd been written off by society. Radical empathy and compassion drove Jesus' decisions as a leader.

Tough leaders are rarely praised for being compassionate, but effective leaders are almost always renowned for their interest in others and their commitment to helping everyone on their teams. Show me a leader with uncommon compassion, and I'll show you an army of people eager to follow that leader into battle.

The best definition of compassion I've heard is simply "*your* pain in *my* heart." When I have compassion for you, I'm feeling your pain in my heart. And I'm making a conscious decision to act on my awareness of your needs. In the first century, the word *compassion* meant more than sympathy for others; it alluded to the visceral yearning we experience in our innermost beings when we have great affection and care for someone.[1]

You see, compassion is empathy in action. While empathy is understanding someone's concerns, compassion is taking on someone else's concerns as your own and doing something about them.

Jesus is without question the most compassionate leader to

ever walk the earth, and how he treated the lonely, the least, and the lost shows us the posture every leader needs.

COMPASSION FOR THE LONELY

When I read Luke 7 for the initial time as a young person, it was one of the first times I felt a true connection with the Jesus of the Bible. As I said, my father died when I was very young. My heart goes out to the woman following the funeral procession in this story because she reminds me of my own widowed mother.

> Jesus went to a town called Nain, and his disciples and a large crowd went along with him. As he approached the town gate, a dead person was being carried out—the only son of his mother, and she was a widow. And a large crowd from the town was with her.[2]

Widows in the first century were vulnerable because they were considered valueless burdens to society. A woman's value in that cultural system was wrapped up in being married and being able to bear children, particularly sons, so that the family inheritance could carry on. Without the agency many women experience today, a childless widow in Jesus' time on earth would quickly become destitute. Perhaps what Luke wants us to see in his storytelling is that the son was not all that died— his mother's future died along with him. She was like a dead woman walking in her son's funeral procession.

Now, although a large crowd surrounded the widow, I believe this mother felt alone. You know, as well as I do, how we can be in a crowded space and still feel alone. The widow of Nain's loneliness touches my heart because my own mother never remarried. She lived isolated for much of her life, which resulted in a lifelong struggle with depression.

How does the Lord react to this scene? He has open eyes to see the woman's pain. He is not too busy to stop and pay attention. Jesus isn't disconnected from or unaware of his people's hardships. No. He's available, aware, and ready to provide an answer to this desperate widow's prayers: "He had compassion for her and said to her, 'Do not weep.'"[3]

Jesus approached the dead son and touched the open coffin, and the pallbearers stopped in their tracks long enough for Christ to command the dead son to get up. Christians are so accustomed to resurrection scenes that I'm afraid we might miss out on the shock of this moment in history: "The dead man sat up and began to speak, and Jesus gave him to his mother."[4]

Isolation is not the way God designed us to flourish. Just look at the New Testament model for life in Christ: The church is designed to be a gathering of people united in their love for one another. Plus, isolation makes us vulnerable and causes us to lose perspective. Notice how the book of Proverbs wisely teaches that isolation is not God's plan for us:

- "There is a path before each person that seems right, but it ends in death."[5]

- "The one who lives alone is self-indulgent, showing contempt for all who have sound judgment."[6]

- "Do you see a man who is wise in his own eyes? There is more hope for a fool than for him."[7]

- "Better is open rebuke than hidden love."[8]
- "As iron sharpens iron, so one person sharpens another."[9]

How in tune are you with your team's needs? When they are struggling, do they feel safe asking for help? Or does your team assume you are too busy or too important to step into their pain? Simply put, leaders need one another. We need a community of Christ-following leaders who will speak truth in love to us when we need exhortation. But that's not possible if we are isolated.

COMPASSION FOR THE LEAST

In Mark's Gospel, Jesus' first recorded miracle involves freeing a demon-possessed man, and this moment is followed by a series of miraculous healings. Mark wants us to define Jesus' leadership in light of his power over demonic forces, unclean spirits, and illness. How does Jesus exert power? How does he prove his unrivaled authority? He shows compassion to the least in a status-driven culture that ranked the sick and unclean at the bottom rung of society.

A man with leprosy approached Jesus on his knees, begging Christ to heal him from a disease that made him an outcast, an untouchable. "Moved with compassion," Scripture tells us, Jesus touched the leper, violating social norms and religious purity.[10] Christ's response to the begging man was to pity his plight and offer him a willingness to heal with these tender words: "I am willing."[11] As you can imagine, after being healed, the man was an effective evangelist for Christ's ministry. Even though Jesus asked the newly healed man to conceal the miracle, the man went out and began to proclaim Jesus' compassion to anyone who would listen.

How many times in our own leadership have people on our teams or in our organizations longed to hear those precious words—*I am willing*? Underneath Jesus' expression of care was a foundation of attention to the needs of others and an interruptible pace of ministry that allowed for this important pause in his journey.

Want to mobilize your team with an unstoppable passion for your mission? Meet their needs. If we're going to lead like Jesus and be easy to follow, we need compassion for everyone.

When our kids, Michael and Jordie, were in grade school, they knew that when my wife and I brought them lunch at school, they could invite one guest to the picnic tables reserved for visiting parents. Nothing brought us more joy and tears than when our kids would choose to invite someone the rest of the kids would label *least* to join us for lunch. Not only was Christ working in Michael's and Jordie's hearts, but we could see God also at work in the hearts of the kids they invited to our table.

My work takes me all over the world to equip leaders, and recently I was privileged to serve a missionary who ministers on a team in South America. There are multiple villages near his home where he has knocked on every single door to share the good news of Jesus Christ. Every. Single. Door. I was so humbled by his tenacity and diligence to share the gospel that I asked if he would coach me in evangelism. What does an effective leader do when someone opens the door to hear the gospel? Number one: He tells everyone, "God sees you." Maybe *you* need to be reminded that God sees you. Even if you'd be considered a "least" leader, you are not alone. The second thing my missionary friend tells people is "Your story matters to God." God is not surprised by your leadership journey. Every circumstance that's come your way, God has either ordained or allowed.

God sees you, and your story matters.

The last thing my friend says to people is "You are loved. You are loved by God, and you are loved by me because of your value to God. You have value."

The leadership path of least resistance is to show favoritism to the people who can benefit you, your mission, and your organization the most. What if instead you and I purposed to become easy-to-follow leaders who take seriously James's message in the second chapter of his epistle: "My brothers and sisters, do not show favoritism as you hold on to the faith in our glorious Lord Jesus Christ"?[12] Every person in your organization needs to hear those three truths: (1) God sees you, (2) your story matters, and (3) you are loved. When we take time to notice and value those we might otherwise overlook, we're leading like Jesus.

COMPASSION FOR THE LOST

Whenever I land in a new city, I jump in a rental car and plug my destination into Google Maps—but I still tend to get lost when I am navigating the road and talking on the phone. This is not the kind of lost I'm referring to, though, when I point out that Jesus has compassion on the lost. The Bible describes lost people as those who will spend the afterlife separated from God if they don't place their faith in Jesus for forgiveness of their sins. People who are lost in the Bible's terms are destined for destruction.

Matthew summarizes Jesus' ministry to the lost like this:

"When he saw the crowds, he had compassion on them because they were confused and helpless, like sheep without a shepherd."[13] *Confused* and *helpless*—two feelings we all try to avoid at all costs, right? Who among us can lead well while burdened with feelings of confusion and helplessness?

That's why clarity is a leader's best friend. Do you feel confused or helpless most of the time at work? Do you think your behavior confuses others or makes them feel helpless? The more you create confusion or leave your team feeling disempowered, the faster you'll perform yourself off a project . . . and maybe off the team altogether. But practice uncommon compassion, and a prerequisite will be creating clarity that diffuses confusion and helplessness (we'll talk more about the *how* of creating clarity in the next chapter).

Any feelings of confusion or helplessness will impact your outcomes. There's no way around it. A leader's goal is to create safe learning environments where everyone is growing personally and professionally. And we simply can't accomplish that without clarity.

Throughout the Gospels we see many examples of Jesus creating clarity for his followers. From the Sermon on the Mount to the Upper Room Discourse, Jesus led his disciples through his teaching in a way that created clarity of purpose and practice. Jesus knew that confused, helpless people act like sheep, hapless animals unable to take care of themselves. But he was on a rescue mission to seek and save the lost. When we prioritize clarity over confusion, we create safe learning environments where everyone is growing, personally and professionally.

Barriers to Compassion

I can already anticipate your hesitations about becoming a more compassionate leader:

- **You're worried that compassionate leadership will lead to coddling underperformers.** But Jesus had no problem calling out sin, leaning into his leaders when they made mistakes, or raising the bar of excellence. Remember the woman caught in adultery? Jesus rescued her from death and covered her shame by distracting the crowd, but he also instructed her to "go and sin no more."[14]

- **You're worried that compassionate leadership will dilute your credibility and passion.** But Jesus sacrificed zero credibility or zeal while practicing care for the people he led. Jesus' strength of mission and message was seen as a threat to the Jewish religious leaders, and it was a source of conviction for many of the sinners who encountered him.

- **You're worried that compassionate leadership will compromise your mission.** For some reason, a lot of leaders believe that the only thing that matters in their organizations is the mission. In this paradigm, leaders are solely focused on their purpose and usually overlook the importance of their methods, giving them plenty of excuses to behave badly. They give little to no thought to how their behaviors influence others. But not only was Jesus intentional about his methods, his mission was also amplified by his tenderness.

- **You're worried that compassionate leadership will make you ineffective.** If you're under the impression that good leadership requires being a jerk, you're wrong. If you're concerned that knowing and addressing the needs of others will bog you down or slow you down, you need to take another look at Jesus. Compassion won't compete with competence; it will amplify it.

Signs You May Struggle with Compassion as a Leader

- **You're disproportionally focused on outcomes.** There's no doubt all leaders must get things done. But not at the expense of the people you're working with or the people you serve.

- **You tend to show favoritism.** It's a common trap for leaders: They spend most of their time with the team members in their organizations who will make their lives easier or the constituents who will affect the bottom line the most.

- **You feel disconnected from people.** You may not be trying to isolate or insulate yourself, but the team around you might experience your leadership as aloof, unreachable, and too busy.

Three Practical Steps toward Creating a Culture of Uncommon Compassion

If you want your team to emulate your behavior, compassion needs to become a cultural value. Here are three practical steps toward creating a culture of uncommon compassion:

1. **Model compassion.** Without taking credit or calling attention to what you're doing, work hard to show others the care you want them to practice.

2. **Celebrate compassion.** When you see people on your team modeling compassion, celebrate their behaviors publicly.

3. **Resource compassion.** Build time into your calendar to spend time with the lonely, the least, and the lost in your organization. Invest time and financial resources in cultivating compassion on your team. Whether that's doing something fun for a few minutes each week or developing connections with one another, resource the behaviors you want to multiply.

GROWING IN COMPASSION

The first people I picture when I think about leaders with uncommon compassion are my dearest friends and ministry partners, Susan and Flip Flippen. I'd been serving under Flip's leadership for less than two years when he emailed about fifty people in his company asking each of us if our mothers were still living. If so, he then asked if we'd give him their addresses so he could send them Mother's Day cards. I assumed he'd purchased a bulk quantity of Mother's Day cards and would have his assistant address the envelopes.

But Flip wrote a personal letter to every living mother of anyone who worked for him. About two years later, when my mother was in hospice and we were having agonizing conversations about end-of-life care and her celebration-of-life ceremony, she pulled out a handwritten note from Flip Flippen. One of my mom's dying wishes was to have Flip's Mother's Day card read out loud during her funeral. Flip's note to her included praise for her investment in my life and the specific ways her leadership affected me and, correspondingly, how my leadership was influencing the Kingdom. I still have the note all these years after her passing.

This is what we learn from Jesus' uncommon compassion for the lonely, the least, and the lost: Seeing people, caring about people, and putting that care into action makes an impact for eternity. To lead with uncommon compassion, we should do these things:

1. **Open our eyes.** Jesus saw the widow, the person with leprosy, and the crowds. We've got to open our eyes to see into the lives of those God has called us to steward through our leadership. To do this, we must slow down,

take some time to really see our people, and engage with them in an authentic and intentional way.

2. **Open our hearts.** Jesus never lacked compassion, even when the people around him were exhausting. Keep your heart open to those around you, even when circumstances make it challenging to do so.

3. **Open our hands.** Without action, compassion is wishful thinking. As a leader, what your people need most from you is openhandedness, a readiness to meet needs when they are presented to you.

How do we do these things practically? Here's what I recommend to increase your compassion for others:

1. **Start listening more.** You can continue to set a high bar without lowering any of your leadership standards, but to become more compassionate, you must listen more to the people around you and seek to understand their needs and challenges.

2. **Start sowing seeds.** The Bible teaches that what we sow we reap—which is another way of saying that there are consequences and benefits to our behaviors. When we invest in others, they will be more willing to invest in the mission of the organization. If you do things for those who could never do anything for you, people will line up to do anything for you. While easy-to-follow leaders don't use compassion to manipulate others, they do discover that compassion becomes a means of motivating others.

You and I can maintain the status quo—the normal, uncaring, disinterested behaviors all too common among good leaders. Or we can become great leaders: the kind who have open hands, hearts, and eyes for the lonely, least, and lost. Let's lead the Jesus way.

PERSONAL REFLECTION QUESTIONS

Write out your answers before you go to bed tonight.

1. When was the last time I disrupted my day to sit and serve another person?

2. Do I have the kind of relationships with my team members where I can ask hard questions?

3. Do my actions match the words that I profess when I talk about the value of each team member and the culture of our organization?

TEAM DISCUSSION QUESTIONS

Ask these questions during your next team meeting.

1. When has someone shown you compassion?
2. Does this team model and reflect the biblical principles of loving our neighbors as ourselves and the Golden Rule of treating others as we would like to be treated?
3. What does retention of our team over recent years say about the compassion of our leadership?

INVITATIONAL QUESTIONS FOR FEEDBACK

Using one of these questions, ask at least one person you lead for feedback in the next seven days.

1. When, if ever, has my leadership made you feel lonely, least, or lost?
2. If you were facing a life challenge or crisis, how likely is it that you'd be willing to be transparent with me about it?
3. How can I best support you and remind you that you are seen, valued, and loved?

SIX

JESUS CLARIFIED HIS EXPECTATIONS

> *"Go and make disciples of all the nations, baptizing them in the name of the Father and the Son and the Holy Spirit. Teach these new disciples to obey all the commands I have given you. And be sure of this: I am with you always, even to the end of the age."*
> JESUS (MATTHEW 28:19-20, NLT)

My professional dream was to become a college basketball head coach. It was a pursuit that I spent hours praying over and preparing for. I had a "dream box" for notes and ideas that I would implement if I ever got the opportunity to coach my own college team.

When that day finally came, I was ready. One of the items in my dream box was a document I had created that outlined one hundred things I would do during my first year as a head coach—important tasks like meeting with the university department chairs, making room in the trophy case, establishing a recruiting pipeline, developing a mantra, promoting camps, and speaking at the Rotary Club. I attacked this cherished opportunity with zeal, more focused on activity than accomplishment.

That first year we had the opportunity to travel to North Carolina for a tournament in the Raleigh-Durham area. True basketball fans know that that's the home of Duke University, which has one of the most successful basketball programs in the history of the game. Our tournament was at another university, but our players wanted to visit Duke's campus and tour their legendary field house, Cameron Indoor Stadium. As our players went into the arena to explore, I decided to enjoy a beautiful late-fall morning outside in the shade of the building.

A few minutes after I sat down, a bus pulled up, and the Duke team walked off. They were returning from a game they had played the night before on the West Coast. I knew they had lost, but even if I hadn't, their body language, facial expressions, and somber tones would have told me.

A friend of one of the players was waiting to give him a ride home, and the conversation I overheard between them changed my life.

"How was the trip to California?" the friend asked.

The player simply responded, "We lost."

The player's friend then tried to turn the conversation back to the trip—how was the weather? Did they see the beach? Again the player responded with "We lost." A couple more attempts followed, but the player's response never wavered: "We lost."

I realized something that morning: Players came to Duke with one simple focus—to win and become champions. Winning was the ultimate pursuit, and anything less was unacceptable.

The focus of that young athlete, half my age, both inspired and challenged me. I was scattered in my focus and distracted by an agenda that promoted busyness over effectiveness. I was leading a competitive college basketball program and yet trying to accomplish a hundred other things; meanwhile, the leaders at Duke, one of the standards of excellence in my sport, focused on only doing one. But what made the difference—what set Duke apart as a champion-level team—was that the focus didn't stay with the leaders. It was clear that they had communicated their expectations so consistently and clearly that their focus had become the identity of the entire program.

I have heard it said that busyness is simply a pursuit of artificial significance. I had fallen victim to that. Have you? Our multiple and varied pursuits may be admirable, but ultimately our job is to create a culture of intentionality and purpose, where the priorities receive the attention and resources that they command. A culture like that can only form when we set clear expectations and align the focus of our whole team.

CONFUSION-FREE ZONE

When I was very young, probably three years old, I found my dad's hammer on the counter near the back door of our house. My dad was always building something, and I wanted to be just like him. So I went into our dining room and started hammering the bookshelves as though I was building them. Hearing the noise, my mother came into the room, saw what I was doing, and exclaimed, "Lyle, use your head!" She said I looked a bit confused for a moment—and then dropped the hammer and started headbutting the shelves.

Have you ever felt like toddler Lyle, following through on an unclear directive but unsure why? Or have you ever felt like you've set the people on your team on a course but somehow sent them headed in a direction that's completely wrong?

That's what happens when we don't communicate our expectations clearly.

Think about your most recent blowup at work. You may feel that you failed or that the team made a mistake—or even worse, you may wonder if you have a people or process problem. Any of those things could be true. But I suspect that the run-of-the-mill hiccups you're facing originate from another source: unmet expectations. You had a picture in your mind of what you desired, a precise vision of what you wanted done. But it didn't happen. You'd thought you'd been crystal clear about a request, but no one on the team followed through. Instead of assuming your people can't or won't deliver, start assuming they lack the clarity they need for excellence. Because here's the thing: What's easy and obvious to you isn't always easy and obvious to others.

The hardest aspects of our role as leaders are not what keep us up at night. We expect difficulty working through conflict, navigating change, making hard choices, and persevering through adversity. We signed up to do hard things. Instead, though, we find ourselves losing sleep over the unanticipated confusion and anxiety these challenges can produce.

Confusion and anxiety are contagious. It only takes one small exposure to something confusing or anxiety inducing before a whole team or project is infected with fear and performance suffers. How do we preempt confusion and anxiety? Set clear expectations. Remember what we learned in the last chapter: Clarity is a leader's best friend. When you create clarity by setting clear expectations, you can quickly eliminate confusion and reduce the fear of the unknown your team may feel.

Even though you're convinced everyone can see things from your point of view—even if you can't imagine something going any other way—no one else but you can know exactly what you're thinking. No one else can picture what you see in your head or understand how important something is to you—unless, of course, you've communicated vision, purpose, goals, and measurables to the point where no one has any questions about their next steps or yours. Easy-to-follow leaders intentionally, ruthlessly clarify their expectations. After all, as Brené Brown wisely notes, "clear is kind."[1]

It won't surprise you at this point to learn that Jesus was a master at setting clear expectations when the stakes were high. Jesus knew that discipleship would come at a cost. When disciples joined Jesus' movement to seek and save the lost, they risked their reputations, social standings, future earnings in their careers, and friendships. They left their homes, families, and careers to go on the road with him. Becoming like Jesus and emulating his leadership became their highest priority.

If we struggle to create clarity about the *what* and *why*, people won't fully engage with the mission. Eliminating ambiguity does more than reduce sideways energy—it also maximizes the energy people bring to what you actually want them to do. When we set clear expectations, we help people get aligned with and excited about the end goal as well as the part they are going to play in getting there. We end up with wholly committed, fully engaged team members operating with straightforward instructions and giving everything they've got to stay on mission.

I believe that's part of the reason Jesus was consistently clear as he helped the disciples understand what was ahead and what the cost would be. Jesus knew that discipleship was going to cost his disciples everything. And he knew it was worth it. He wanted them to be perfectly clear on both points.

HOW JESUS SET EXPECTATIONS

Much of leading others is communicating expectations and holding others accountable to the standards set, which means that learning how to zone in on what really matters is key. Jesus knew how to level someone's expectations and clarify his own. And he didn't use force, shame, or pressure to reach clarity. He was winsome and firm.

Jesus' Sermon on the Mount is his most famous teaching, and like with much of what we're familiar with in Scripture, it can be easy to miss the leadership implications in what he's doing. As we revisit his words, we'll discover Jesus' masterful way of creating, maintaining, and multiplying clarity: by being precise, practical, and persistent.

JESUS IS PRECISE

At the beginning of the Sermon on the Mount Jesus gives his listeners nine simple truths that have come to be known as the Beatitudes.[2] Each one is communicated in a simple yet very precise pattern:

Blessed are _____,

for _____

_____.

Those who mourn will be comforted. Those who hunger and thirst for righteousness will be satisfied. Jesus has provided a brilliant template for leaders to use to elevate our communication: Define the behaviors you desire and the resulting benefits. Those who consistently meet deadlines will earn a higher degree of empowerment. Those who demonstrate initiative and follow-through will be trusted and receive more responsibility.

JESUS IS PRACTICAL

In Matthew 6, Jesus addresses three simple, practical behaviors that he expects each of his followers to emulate: give, pray, and fast. He doesn't say "if" you give, pray, or fast; he says "when" you give, pray, and fast. The beauty of these instructions is in the attention to detail that Jesus uses in setting his expectations. In each case, Jesus communicates (1) what he wants his followers to do, (2) the way he wants them to do it, and (3) why it is important to do it that way. For example, when Jesus talks about prayer, he tells the disciples to pray privately and succinctly and that the Father will reward them. As leaders, this pattern of sharing the *what*, the *way*, and the *why* of our expectations will help create clarity.

JESUS IS PERSISTENT

Whenever Jesus taught in a form other than the parable, he made his point evident and consistent. Throughout the Sermon on the Mount, Jesus circles back to the central theme of his ministry: his mission to seek and save the lost. He uses a variety of word pictures, like that of entering through a narrow gate or building a house on a rock, to illustrate and encourage his listeners to seek first the Kingdom of God.

As a leader, are your messages this pointed? Do you communicate your mission, values, and expectations with clarity and consistency?

Jesus' parables demonstrate a persistence to develop understanding in his listeners in a way that transcends a direct message. Over time I have come to learn that the mind thinks in pictures. When I speak of love to my congregation, my mind immediately goes to either a Hallmark couple holding hands at sunset or my Savior, Jesus, on the cross. Or have you ever noticed that when we tell young children not to spill the milk oftentimes we clean up a spill a couple of minutes later? The reason is that we put the picture of spilling in their minds. Jesus was persistent in teaching using parables because they created word pictures that aligned with the message he was attempting to communicate.

Leaders with Clear Expectations	Leaders without Clear Expectations
lead teams with highly engaged members who have clarity on the *what*, *way*, and *why*	create confusion and frustration because the strategic path is unclear or doesn't exist
energize their teams with a well-defined vision and compelling desired outcomes	try "random acts of improvement" and multiple new initiatives at the same time that don't align with any meaningful goals or strategy
align resources—like time, people, and money—toward meaningful projects and processes	hire quality talent but have a hard time retaining team members due to a high degree of frustration and a lack of traction toward significant outcomes
see team members fully empowered and flourishing	sometimes become toxic as frustrations are shared and failures begin to compound

Please remember this, leader: What is easy and obvious to us isn't always easy and obvious to those we lead. To engage and elevate our people, we must commit to an uncommon level of clarity in how we set expectations with each person and in every conversation.

How to Set Clear Expectations

1. Write down your expectations and read them aloud. If they don't make sense to you, they will never make sense to others. Use word pictures and tangible examples. For instance, instead of using the term *respect*, create a word picture such as "Treat everyone like they are first-time guests in your home."

2. Set an appointed time for a group discussion and decide in advance what you are going to say.

3. Determine the most important next step using the *what*, *way*, and *why* framework.

4. If there is a deadline or a frequency desired for a specific behavior, be sure to articulate it.

5. Summarize by defining why an expectation is important and how it aligns with the mission.

PERSONAL REFLECTION QUESTIONS
Write out your answers before you go to bed tonight.

1. Am I leading my team with the precision, practicality, and persistence they deserve?

2. What percentage of my communication is proactive? Am I spending my time in instruction or in frustration? If I am being overly reactive, how can I take steps to reduce that?

3. Can I clearly articulate what high performance looks like in my organization?

TEAM DISCUSSION QUESTIONS

Ask these questions during your next team meeting.

1. What are the three most important things you do here?
2. What does winning look like for this team?
3. When you joined this team, was your onboarding experience sufficient? Why or why not?

INVITATIONAL QUESTIONS FOR FEEDBACK

Using one of these questions, ask at least one person you lead for feedback in the next seven days.

1. What rhythms of communication and clarity of expectations would I need to provide to make this a *world-class* work experience?
2. Do you have an example of when I wasn't precise, practical, or persistent in my communication with you?
3. On a scale of 1 to 10 (with 1 meaning "virtually nonexistent" and 10 meaning "extremely high"), what is your frustration level in your current role? Why?

SEVEN

JESUS CULTIVATED GENEROSITY

Let the same mind be in you that was in Christ Jesus,
  who, though he was in the form of God,
    did not regard equality with God
    as something to be exploited,
  but emptied himself,
    taking the form of a slave,
    being born in human likeness.
  And being found in human form,
    he humbled himself
    and became obedient to the point of death—
    even death on a cross.

PHILIPPIANS 2:5-8, NRSV

Let me start this story with two numbers: $27 billion and seven times. A few years ago, I was given a gift card for a hundred dollars to a local retailer. I travel frequently, so I may go months without visiting any local stores or businesses in my community. However, in time, I do like to get out to our local businesses and support them. It had been many months since I had received my gift card, but finally one Saturday I went out excited to shop.

I browsed the store, picked out a few items, and headed over to the checkout. The young clerk scanned my items, and when it came time for payment, I proudly presented my gift card. The clerk tried to input the gift card into their system, but it was rejected. He tried again—another rejection. After a little bit of research, he informed me that the gift card had expired. I guess I'd had it for more than just a few months!

As I reached for my wallet, the clerk looked at me and said, "You must be new to our store. I don't recognize you." I told him yes, it was my first visit; I had received the gift card shortly after the store had opened but hadn't had the chance to come by until today. I then handed him my credit card, but to my surprise he chose not to accept it. He said, "I am happy that you chose to come in, and I am going to honor the gift card even though it is expired. I think it's more important to have a new customer than it is to adhere to our standard procedure."

A 2024 study concluded that there is about $27 billion on unused gift cards in the United States.[1] My gift card to this store was destined to become part of that statistic. Instead, the store employee decided to be gracious and generous. He was under no obligation to do so; he simply decided to put a potential long-term customer over a store policy.

His generosity has been rewarded many times over, in a variety of ways. When I need items that are sold in that store, I always purchase from them, even when an online purchase would be less expensive and more convenient. More importantly, I have become an apostle for this business. I tell friends, family, people in my church, and even strangers about this great store. The generosity demonstrated by the clerk that day by honoring my hundred-dollar gift card has produced hundreds of dollars of revenue from my loyalty and thousands of dollars of revenue from my reviews and recommendations to others.

What's the cost of lacking generosity? According to an oft-cited marketing study, 95 percent of people surveyed admit they've told others about a negative customer service experience.[2] That makes sense to me. There have been many times when I have encountered a stingy, bottom-line-only business that places profits over people and shows no grace in their return policies, cancellation rules, or customer service practices. These businesses trade a short-term gain for what could potentially be thousands of dollars of lost revenue due to unfavorable word-of-mouth testimonies and online reviews.

The choice to be generous is like throwing a rock into a pond: one big splash followed by multiple ripples. Generosity always makes a big initial impact but then is followed by other positive, though less obvious, effects. Any act of generosity is both impactful and inspiring. Are you creating positive ripples in your family, business, church, and community through a generous lifestyle of open hands and an open heart? Or are you prone to closing your mind and your fists, choosing instead an abundance of greed and an absence of grace?

CULTIVATING GENEROSITY

One of the greatest honors of my life has been to witness godly leaders sending monetary gifts across the world to support missions globally. Very recently I keynoted an event that raised millions of dollars to support discipleship in over two hundred countries. While these initiatives are making a Kingdom impact and serve as an example of bighearted and openhanded

Signs of a Generous Leader	Signs of a Stingy Leader
Their coworkers, ministry partners, and loved ones are well cared for and have their needs met.	**They usually suffer from** isolation, perfectionism, regret, resentment, keeping score, and a fixed mindset.
They are humble. Generous leaders focus on the needs of others rather than themselves.	**Their vocabulary is the unholy trinity: *I, me, my.*** If a leader usually finds a way to point back to themselves, focus on only their goals, or use the words *I, me,* and *my* often, they're not generous.
They retain great leaders in their organizations. Generous leaders usually have a lot of loyal people staying in their organizations for the long haul because everyone wants to work with, for, or around generous people.	**They are transactional in relationships and conversations.** You know the feeling you get when someone is talking through, around, or over you but not with you? That's a transactional conversation that always leads to transactional relationships: You scratch my back; I'll scratch yours. Jesus didn't lead like this.
They are peace filled. Generous leaders don't focus only on numbers or abstract goals; they are busy elevating others and finding ways to help everyone on their teams find greater satisfaction at work.	**They are bitter or cynical.** Keeping score is exhausting, and keeping a record of wrongs is a foolproof way to become resentful and selfish. Becoming a generous leader means letting others off the hook, wiping the slate clean, and valuing forgiveness and grace over being right.
Their organizations are healthy. Generous leaders are others-centric, always looking through a window at the needs of the people around them instead of looking in the mirror.	**They want to be judged by their intentions, not their actions.** Stingy leaders throw up defenses when they are held accountable and often try to deflect constructive feedback by blaming their actions and celebrating their intentions. Generous leaders don't shift the blame from their actions to their intentions; they take radical ownership, apologize, and change.

stewardship, donating money is not the only way to cultivate generosity. When we talk about becoming generous leaders, we need to broaden our imagination beyond dropping a tithe into an offering plate, scanning a QR code to support a charity of our choice, or financially investing in those we lead.

Yes, supporting the local and global church has significant Kingdom impact. Giving your team raises and compensating your leaders unselfishly are tangible ways to remind them of their value to the team. But financial gifts are only one of many ways to give of yourself in a way that mirrors Jesus' self-giving love.

In our church offices, the first thing we see each morning as we enter is a large sign that has Micah 6:8 painted in big, bold letters. We are reminded to "act justly and to love mercy and to walk humbly with [our] God." This reminder—to actively love and serve others out of our humble walk with God—helps me define generosity: a worldview or lifestyle where we value others more than we value ourselves.

Generosity is the idea that *this is not about me*. A generous leader puts a high value on the people around them at work and makes every effort to ensure they are cared for materially, financially, and emotionally. This kind of generosity makes you an easy-to-follow leader.

Jesus is the epitome of generosity, and yet he had very few material possessions during his time on earth. Most of his disciples lived frugally as members of a lower socioeconomic status. But from his birth and through his crucifixion and resurrection, Jesus' life was one continuous act of generosity. Christ propelled his followers toward immeasurable and illogical generosity because they were motivated to be like him.

For many leaders today, promotions, titles, and influence can cause entitlement, manipulation, and selfishness to creep into our lives. But Jesus led in a countercultural way: with generous humility, love, and selflessness.

GENEROUS HUMILITY

Many times, leaders who've had high performance metrics, received much acclaim, or seem to shine in comparison to others fall under the pretense that they're above others. Unfortunately, I've had a front-row seat to leaders who grumble with discontentment, whine about the special treatment their success should afford them, and resist any form of accountability. This kind of behavior is hard to follow, self-serving, opportunistic, dangerous, and in extreme cases predatory. Anything that starts with an attitude of entitlement—with *I*, *me*, or *my*—won't propel a team or organization forward. Self-focused leaders build self-serving empires that diminish others and become misaligned and impotent in pursuing the original mission.

The truth of the gospel of Jesus Christ should stop entitlement in its tracks. You and I are sinners saved only by grace. Our brokenness deserves condemnation. And that means we are not entitled to anything. This is especially hard for leaders to grasp when they've climbed a corporate ladder and reached the top, served in high-capacity roles in the nonprofit or ministry world, and/or gained an influential following with a large platform—and that is where looking at Jesus' leadership can correct our perspective.

In his letter to the church at Philippi, the apostle Paul wrote that we should "adopt the same attitude as that of Christ Jesus, who, existing in the form of God, did not consider equality with God as something to be exploited."[3] Jesus didn't exploit the fact that he was one of three persons of the Holy Trinity. No, he humbled himself. If we're going to lead with hearts of generosity like Jesus', we must understand that we can't live with entitlement or dwell on what we think we deserve.

Generosity is both an attitude and a posture of humility. Basketball coach John Wooden said, "A gentleman is one who considers the rights of others before his own feelings, and the feelings of others before his own rights."[4] The same could be said about a generous leader: Generous leaders humbly consider the needs and rights of others before their personal feelings and the feelings of others before their personal rights and needs.

GENEROUS LOVE

Whenever we went out to eat as our kids were growing up, there was always a moment when they became selfless and animated—and it was right about when we would start to discuss the possibility of ordering dessert. No two people have ever displayed the gift of encouragement more than when our kids would prompt my wife or me to order something sweet. "You deserve it!" they would tell us. "It's your favorite!" they would urge. In reality, they wanted us to order dessert because they would get to share it with us. Their words were kind and generous—and emerged from a desire to get something for themselves.

Sadly, lots of leaders still think that giving is the best way to get. Whether they are trying to manipulate God or trying to manipulate another leader or situation, immature leaders believe generosity is transactional and not relational. Leaders who give to get are always consumed with keeping score and a record of wrongs.

In contrast, mature, godly leaders give sacrificially because they are motivated by love. They don't give to get; they give because they love. Easy-to-follow leaders empty themselves as servants to others in the same way Christ offered himself to us.

John the apostle tells us in 1 John 4:19 that "we love because he first loved us." The root of manipulative leadership is self-preservation. The root of generous leadership is love. If we want to cultivate more generosity, we should be the kind of people who are practiced at receiving God's love, who surrender to living and leading loved.

We are not the source of our growth; God is. If you're tripping over yourself to love others—and I have a hunch that many of the leaders reading this book are—maybe you haven't fully embraced your identity as a beloved child of God. Because once you receive God's love, you can offer it to others.

To understand what God's extravagant, deeply sacrificial love looks like, we should consider the sacrificial love a healthy parent has for their child. Kids may never recognize or appreciate parental sacrifices. And there's no guarantee kids will love their parents back. But sacrificial parents love anyway. How they parent—how they lead—is motivated by generous love.

In the same way, loving others generously is the outcome of brimming with God's sacrificial, parental love. Because God is generous, he gave up the one thing that he only had one of: his Son. *That's* how valuable you are. *That's* how much God loves you. How might that kind of love expand your generosity as you lead?

GENEROUS SELFLESSNESS

A few years back, I spoke at a conference in New York City, and the following morning I went for a run in Central Park. On my way back to the hotel, I spotted a beautiful Methodist church building. Since I love old churches, I poked my head in to see what it looked like inside. I never would have done so if I'd known there was a service going on, but there I was, sweaty and out of breath, trying to get through the courtyard gate into the building. Before I reached the sanctuary, a woman approached me and introduced herself, asking where I was from.

She asked if I was going to attend the church service, and I was tempted to look myself up and down and point to the sweat dripping off my athletic clothes. Although I can imagine what I must have looked like to that woman, I can't imagine what I smelled like. I said, "Oh no, ma'am. I was just going to look at the building. I'm a Christian, I'm a brother in Christ, but you don't want me to come in there."

And she said, "I'd be so disappointed if you didn't."

As self-conscious as I felt finding a seat in the circle huddled in the sanctuary, I couldn't stop thinking about the selflessness of this woman in actively recruiting me into the church—not thinking of her own comfort or the church's image but wanting me to know I belonged. As much as I wanted to hide, I also felt loved. She'd been generous with her invitation, and it wasn't lost on me how easy it would have been for her to be passive about the whole situation. Instead, her selfless initiative blessed me.

By the end of the service, the church was filled with people who appeared to be experiencing homelessness and several others who had gone without showers for a lot longer than me, all of whom this woman had actively welcomed inside. What a beautiful example of God's grace and goodness, a fragrant reminder that we really are actively welcomed and pursued by God.

Generosity actively serves. Generosity is selflessness in action. The absence of generosity reveals something about our own hearts.

Think about the last time you hurt someone with your words or actions. Or your biggest leadership failure. I suspect that if you are honest in your evaluation, you will notice two critical mistakes:

1. You allowed self to become the focus.
2. Your selfishness caused you to veer away from the path of generosity.

Selfless generosity is why Jesus "humbled himself by becoming obedient to death—even death on a cross!"[5] Jesus' generosity was never more active, more focused on serving the desperate needs of those who could not help themselves, than in his death on the cross. Jesus' leadership shows us that generosity is not passive. It's active.

Leader, if we pursue opportunities to be generous, we must expect that the price we pay will be sacrificial. If Jesus is active, if he pursues and seeks the lost so that he can sacrifice for those in need, so should we.

GENEROUS WITH MUCH AND LITTLE

The most generous leader I know is Natalie Halbert. I've had the distinguished honor of serving with Natalie on a church staff, and I've witnessed firsthand the lengths she will go to to be generous. Natalie brings an abundance to her work—not just blessings like a fantastic support system and the respect of the community but also wit, intelligence, skills, and experience. She's brimming with so much to offer others, and she does it with humility, love, and selflessness. In all the years we've partnered together in leadership, I can't remember a time she's resorted to anything that communicates *I, me,* or *my.* She is always mindful of the impact our initiatives have on the whole team, always eager to make someone else's dreams come true or help someone else reach their goal. I joke with Natalie that I

> **Three Checks for the Generous Leader**
> 1. **Perspective check.** When we are interrupted by others, do we consider that an obligation or an opportunity? The greatest gift you'll ever give another human being is your full attention. Look at Jesus in the Gospels: He stops, he kneels, he weeps, he touches—he never fails to give people his full attention. Do a perspective check. Do the people in the organization where you lead seem like obligations or opportunities?
>
> 2. **Purpose check.** When we give to others, do we expect to get things in return? Do we have an agenda? Ask yourself, *Why am I* really *doing this? Am I looking to gain anything out of this?*
>
> 3. **Process check.** Generosity is not something we do. It needs to become who we are. Ask yourself, *Is generosity just something I do, or am I truly becoming a generous leader?*

want her to sign a lifetime contract. I truly never want to work on a team that doesn't include her. Of course, part of that desire is due to *what* she brings to our team: Her talents and tenacity are a blessing. But the greater impact of her work is the *way* she does it—serving and championing others to help them learn, grow, and achieve extraordinary outcomes.

The beauty of working with someone like Natalie is that their generosity rubs off on you and the rest of the team. Generosity is culture making.

But generosity doesn't just show up in abundance. Remember, generosity is *a worldview or lifestyle where we value others more than we value ourselves*. That means we give what we have—whatever we have—for the sake of others.

There's no better illustration of this than the penniless widow in Luke 21. Usually leaders assume that generosity overflows from abundance, but this poor but generous widow shows us how to lead with benevolence.

The destitute widow comes to the Temple to donate two small coins to God, even though it is all she has to offer. She puts herself in a position where faith is her only option. Either God will come through or she will perish. She truly gives it all, not out of manipulation or desperation but out of surrender.

Ultimately, generosity is an act of surrender.

Leader, are you totally surrendered to God? Are you holding out, keeping your options open, or resigned to treating God like a last resort? Maybe you used to be a more generous person. But life, ministry, and disappointment have a way of hardening our hearts and closing us off, don't they? I've been there many times myself. That's no way to live or lead. Especially in light of the access you have to God through Christ and the ongoing presence of the Holy Spirit. Follow the example of the poor widow and offer God all you have, then do the same with everyone you work alongside. Let God soften your heart as you reflect on his abundant generosity toward you. Let him lead you back to the generous person you truly can be.

Give what you have. Give it all.

PERSONAL REFLECTION QUESTIONS

Write out your answers before you go to bed tonight.

1. Who is the most selfless leader I know? How close am I to being compared to that leader? What about that person would I like to emulate?

2. Do I have a heart for the same things God has a heart for?

3. Am I threatened by the success or status of other leaders?

TEAM DISCUSSION QUESTIONS

Ask these questions during your next team meeting.

1. When have you felt loved by me?
2. When have you felt most valued and appreciated by me?
3. Do we have a culture where the needs of team members are identified and addressed?

INVITATIONAL QUESTIONS FOR FEEDBACK

Using one of these questions, ask at least one person you lead for feedback in the next seven days.

1. Do you feel like you are getting appropriate credit for the work you do?
2. Have there been times when you have felt that my agenda or ambitions have been selfish and counterproductive to the mission of our team?
3. In what ways could I be more generous to you? My time? My resources? My empathy?

EIGHT

JESUS EMPOWERED OTHERS

"I tell you the truth, anyone who believes in me will do the same works I have done, and even greater works, because I am going to be with the Father."
JESUS (JOHN 14:12, NLT)

Whenever I share about the concept of empowerment, I tell this story.

It was a busy evening at Los Angeles International Airport, a place few airports can rival in flight and customer volume. Standing in line, waiting to see a customer service representative of one of the nation's largest airlines, was a prominent, successful entrepreneur. Behind him was a good friend of mine, a regional sales representative from Texas.

A window opened, and the prominent entrepreneur stepped up and began to share his need with the young customer service representative. In moments my friend started to notice a bit of energy from the prominent businessman. Evidently, what this gentleman wanted was not possible. As the customer service representative tried to explain that the request was not feasible, the entrepreneur started to up his energy, making statements like "Do you know who I am?," "You don't understand who you are talking to," and "I will have your job if you can't make this happen!"

This commotion went on for another few minutes, but ultimately the entrepreneur resigned himself to his fate and accepted the alternative option, checked his luggage, and walked away, muttering comments about never flying with this airline again.

Through the entire incident, the young woman who served the obnoxious man maintained her poise and was exceptionally professional. My friend had witnessed the entire exchange, and when he was called to the window he stepped up and immediately began to affirm the young customer service rep. He complimented her graciousness under fire, her patience, and her resilience in not bowing to the unreasonable demands of the previous customer.

My friend's words were immediately met with resistance. The young woman was quick to deflect the affirmations and asked my friend to please stop with the commendations. He was a little confused by this, but she quickly clarified why she was reluctant to receive the praise. She said, "I appreciate your kindness, but what I did really doesn't deserve your compliments." She then added this caveat: "What I did isn't commendable. You see, the man who was angry is flying to Chicago tonight, but he made me mad, so I am sending his luggage to Newark!"

Obviously, the turn in this story is a crowd-pleaser and always results in a great laugh. To my knowledge this story is an urban myth, and I confess to my groups that it isn't factual, but it does illustrate the difference between people who are empowered and those who aren't.

The businessman in this story appears empowered—he is wealthy, has status on the airline, and is used to having people concede to his demands. But in this scenario he ultimately has no power. The customer service representative seems like a victim early in the story, but when it comes to decision making, she holds all the cards.

Empowerment can be granted in a variety of ways. In this story, empowerment is positional: The customer service rep can ultimately determine what flight the businessman is on and where his luggage will go. In other situations, a person may be empowered legally or even relationally. In any of these circumstances, the level of empowerment will determine the amount of impact an individual may have.

Are you a leader who strives to empower others, giving them permission to live and perform at their highest and best? Or are you a minimizer, a leader who offers few opportunities for others to learn, grow, and change?

SKILLS AND PERMISSION

One of the most empowering leaders I have ever had the privilege of meeting is Mike Krzyzewski, a former basketball coach at Duke University. During his coaching career, Coach K's teams won over twelve hundred games, five national championships, and three Olympic gold medals.[1] His coaching résumé is one of the most impressive for any coach in any sport ever.

But Coach K didn't become a coach just to win games. His objective—what he considered his primary role as a leader—was to influence and develop young men. He wanted to empower his players to develop the attributes that would make them effective leaders in their future endeavors, be they in athletics, business, education, or even ministry. Coach K once stated,

> Leadership isn't a flowchart or report or algorithm or a committee. It's about giving people room to grow because everyone changes on your team, even when it's the same people. They change and grow.[2]

Leadership that leaves a lasting mark includes empowerment. Although *empowerment* can be an overused leadership buzzword—usually misunderstood and often carelessly applied—it is also an essential element in the leadership toolbox of anyone who aspires to be easy to follow.

Here's how I define empowerment: *the appropriate relationship between skills, opportunity, and permission*. Empowerment requires knowing each person on your team, understanding their skills and capacity, and making sure they know you have their backs.

Balancing skills, opportunity, and permission is key. Leaders will grant a level of permission that far exceeds a team member's ability, resulting in feelings of frustration and overwhelm. Or leaders can tell a skilled team member that they have permission but then not provide an opportunity for that person to use those skills. Leaders can also misuse or even abuse their power if they delegate responsibility without granting any actual authority. True empowerment gives permission and support in responsibilities fully in line with a person's skills.

If you're feeling overwhelmed, teetering on the brink of

burnout, exhibiting control tendencies, complaining about team performance, or feeling lost in the weeds, learning the artful behaviors of empowerment could relieve you of burdens you were never meant to carry alone. With the right empowerment strategy, you and your team can transition from *task-oriented* leadership to *people-focused* leadership, which makes burnout less likely to occur and fosters personal development and team member engagement. Empowerment is the difference between creating a culture of micromanagement and minimization and cultivating a culture of trust and multiplication.

HOW JESUS EMPOWERED

To truly empower, we have to give others the skills, opportunities, and permission they need to expand their own credibility and influence. If leadership is about moving people and processes forward, we cannot lead people to a new level of experience, effectiveness, or efficiency if we are not willing to empower them.

The beauty of Jesus is that his ministry was not about gaining power and attention himself; rather, it was about including and empowering others. Through Jesus' life and ministry, we discover that empowerment can be broken down into three fundamental questions:

1. **Can this person do what is required?** For a person to be empowered appropriately, they must be given opportunities that match the skills they have. I have flown over two million miles in my adult life, but if I walked onto an airplane and the pilot offered me the opportunity to fly the plane, the appropriate response would be an

emphatic no. Although I have logged hours upon hours as a passenger, I have zero skills as a pilot.

Jesus spent three years teaching, training, and guiding his disciples. I love that when Jesus fed the multitudes his response to the disciples' concerns was "You give them something to eat."[3] We all know that the miraculous multiplication came from Jesus, but the Lord made sure the disciples participated in all the ways they could.

2. **Should this person do what is required?** Empowerment is not just a matter of what a person *can* do; it also involves utilizing an appropriate opportunity for them to do it. I have been driving automobiles for over four decades with a minimal number of tickets and only a couple of fender benders. By all metrics I am a good driver—my insurance company says so! However, when I travel to other countries, I rarely—if ever—drive a car. I am a proven and skilled driver, but a new country means new traffic laws and unfamiliar traffic patterns. In many countries the driver sits on the opposite side of the car and the car is intended to be driven on the opposite side of the road! I may have the skill to drive, but the opportunity comes with further obstacles.

When Jesus sent the twelve apostles out on their first missionary journey, he did so knowing that he had developed in them the skills to do what he asked. However, he suggested they use discernment regarding opportunity: "If anyone does not welcome you or listen to your words, shake the dust off your feet when you leave that house or town."[4] In other words, he was giving them guidance about how to identify the right and wrong opportunities for using their skills.

3. **Am I giving this person the support they need to do what is required?** If a person can and should do a particular task or embrace a specific assignment, the leader's final step is giving permission—letting that person know that the leader has their back and is supporting them in what they do with the assignment. When the time, setting, and opportunity are right, a leader's permission gives the green light with both blessing and encouragement.

   In Matthew 28 we see Jesus take this final step of empowerment, offering his blessing and encouragement to his disciples in what we now call the great commission. Jesus is affirming that the disciples can go, teach, and baptize. Jesus is also communicating that this is something they should *now* go and do. And finally, we see his blessing and encouragement as he shares with them that he will be "with [them] always, to the very end of the age."[5]

Ultimately, as Jesus models, the goal of empowerment is to help people grow to a place where they can perform at a level equal to or better than the leader. Empowering others multiplies impact. Jesus invested in and developed twelve apostles and then empowered them to "go and make disciples of all nations."[6] Coach K influenced hundreds of players in his forty-two years at Duke, and those players went on to become significant leaders of thousands of other people. How many leaders have you developed and then released into significant roles with big responsibilities?

Characteristics of Empowering Leaders

- **They are humble.** Only a selfless leader would consider developing those around them to such a degree that one day they may surpass that leader. In John 14:12, Jesus encourages his disciples by saying that one day they will do greater works than him.

- **They are available.** It takes time and lots of conversations to truly empower others. Jesus was with his disciples almost nonstop for three years. An empowering leader is available for the critical questions and conversations that grow others.

- **They are transparent.** An empowering leader must be willing to become vulnerable and real with their followers. For a person to become truly skilled, they must understand not only what to do but also the cost and commitment required. Jesus showed his disciples his strength in the miracles he performed, but he also showed his hurts and his disappointments. His disciples knew the work that was ahead of them because Jesus was transparent as he trained them.

- **They are patient.** Developing skills in others can be a time-intensive, sometimes frustrating process. Jesus often had to explain parables or bring additional clarity to his teaching. He did this with empathy and grace. Even in his restoration of Peter we see Jesus teaching and refining one of his closest friends, preparing him for the empowerment that was about to come.

- **They are courageous.** The risk of failure is always present when a leader trusts others through the act of empowerment. In my own leadership journey, I often have to challenge my own fear of failure, reminding myself that the leaders who shaped me trusted me, even if my initial results were subpar. Courageous leaders trust the process but also trust that God will walk alongside those they empower.

My grandfather was the chief of police in a resort town that had a famous amusement park. Since my mom was a teacher and had summers off, we'd spend our entire summer in my grandfather's hometown. As a kid I would be at the park for hours every day, taking rides, dominating Skee-Ball, and eating endless hot dogs and ice cream cones.

As I grew older, though, my grandfather wanted me to start learning responsibility. The summer I was twelve, he arranged for me to work at a mini-golf course, covering the lunch and dinner hours for the older lady who owned it. Then, at thirteen, I added being there in the morning to help her open and in the evening to help her close. As I developed a better knowledge of the operation and gained skills in dealing with the tourists, my responsibilities and opportunities became greater. The summer I turned fourteen, I was offered the opportunity to run the course alone, working ten-hour days and being completely responsible for the facility, the equipment, and the customers. (I will humbly confess that cute girls often played for free!)

I am sure some labor laws were bent, but I was given the skills, the opportunity, and ultimately the permission to be a small-business operator at the age of fourteen. I worked hard each evening to make sure that the money in the cash register was balanced, and I proudly kept track of the number of customers we served each day. That experience was a great training ground for a boy who would one day run a college athletic department, lead thriving churches, and build businesses of his own.

Empowering is giving people steady, deliberate opportunities to grow. When leaders empower well, the people who work with them flourish.

The Costs of Not Empowering Our Teams

I know that many leaders say that they empower others but actually don't. They cite reasons like "My team can't do it as well as I can" or "It takes too much time to develop these skills in others, so it is quicker to do it myself." I can certainly understand this line of thinking, but in the end, it is foolish and even potentially fatal to an organization. Failure to empower can become very costly. At first the cost is in time: A leader who won't empower will find that their time is being consumed by either doing tasks that others potentially can and should be doing or by going back to fix issues that were created by others who were never taught to perform the tasks correctly. Leaders who won't empower eventually end up exhausted and exasperated.

The second cost that will eventually come to pass is talent. High-performing people thrive in roles where they feel valued by being empowered. A leader who refuses to empower others may attract talent, but those high performers will quickly experience the frustration of not being empowered and will look for roles in other organizations where they will be given authority and shown appreciation.

In the same way that parenting models the love God has for us, how parents build into their kids is also a great example of empowerment. I don't know any loving parent who wouldn't be thrilled to see their children become more successful than them. We beam with pride and glow with joy when our kids get good grades, excel in extracurricular activities, and demonstrate maturity far beyond their years. We aren't jealous of their achievements, because our goal is their success. Our entire parenting process is one of empowerment. We teach our kids to walk, then to ride a bike, and eventually to drive a car. We train them to make the bed and eventually teach them how to live on their own.

I was extremely fortunate to have a grandfather and a mother who understood the practice of empowerment and gave me both the opportunity and the encouragement to grow, dare, and mature.

That same attitude is present in an empowering leader. Empowerment begins with humility and genuine love for those we serve. We long to see those we lead thrive and excel. Only a truly humble leader is willing to develop other leaders and deploy them to accomplish great things.

PERSONAL REFLECTION QUESTIONS

Write out your answers before you go to bed tonight.

1. Do I treat my emerging leaders, and the leaders I serve under, the way I want to be treated?

2. How do other people experience my leadership?

3. If I had the opportunity to work for a boss like me, would I? Why or why not?

TEAM DISCUSSION QUESTIONS

Ask these questions during your next team meeting.

1. What gifts and talents are not being leveraged fully right now?
2. Does everyone on the team have the permission and empowerment they need?
3. What can we do to cultivate a greater sense of ownership in each role for all the members of our team?

INVITATIONAL QUESTIONS FOR FEEDBACK

Using one of these questions, ask at least one person you lead for feedback in the next seven days.

1. Am I the kind of leader who rolls out the red carpet to empower you to take on more responsibilities and risks or the kind who pulls the rug out from under you?
2. Describe the last time you felt completely empowered to do your best work—a time you were fully trusted in your role. What was that experience like for you?
3. What skills do you possess that you believe are going unrecognized or underutilized?

A FINAL QUESTION

ARE YOU EASY TO FOLLOW?

"I am the light of the world. Whoever follows me will never walk in darkness, but will have the light of life."
JESUS (JOHN 8:12)

On a road trip up the New England coast, I got the chance to visit several charming historic lighthouses, and I was wowed by their beauty and practicality. Not only did every lighthouse have a unique and striking architectural design, but each one also had a distinct story regarding its origin, design, and impact on the safety and security of the sailors who benefited from its function.

What struck me most about the stories were the three things they had in common:

1. Lighthouses are **established intentionally**. Each one was placed in a precise geographic location, a place where its light could be seen from the greatest distance possible.

2. Lighthouses **exist to serve**. Although many of these lighthouses are now landmarks and tourist attractions, the original goal of their existence was to serve others, not to draw attention to themselves.

3. Lighthouses **exist to guide** those who need navigation or rescue. Long before someone could schedule an Uber on their phone or pull up directions with an app, sailors were wholly dependent upon lighthouses to guide them away from treacherous shores. With light to guide them, sailors could identify their own location and navigate along the coast; this light therefore prevented shipwrecks and helped travelers reach their ports at night or during storms.

Although I stayed on a tight budget throughout my bucket-list trip to New England, I did go a little overboard buying lighthouse souvenirs at nearly every gift shop along the shores. I've kept those little lighthouses as enduring symbols of the challenges and triumphs easy-to-follow leaders face when they are tossed back and forth between the waves of leadership.

I see lighthouses as a beaming picture of Jesus' leadership and what it looks like to become a guiding light to others as they navigate the choppy waters of leadership. Noticing the three simple commonalities inspired me to create the term *lighthouse leader*. Like these amazing structures, lighthouse leaders are easy to follow because

1. they intentionally lead, so their behaviors become a model for all to see,

2. they are focused on serving others, and
3. they provide lessons and encouragement to help others navigate lives that may be filled with storms and riptides.

Leaders who aren't easy to follow are more like stoplights than lighthouses. When you serve under stoplight leaders, you're likely following their leadership with caution and hesitation—braking every few weeks in anticipation of their changing lights instead of fully pursuing your passion and calling. Even more challenging is following a lights-out leader who creates confusion for everyone around them. Lights-out leaders make people feel like they are lost in the dark—as though they are at sea at night along rocky shores in unpredictable weather.

In contrast, easy-to-follow leaders are fully dedicated to helping others find their way to purpose and calling. Like lighthouses, they intentionally change their behaviors to become guides, helping others navigate the treacherous waters of leadership as they form their own unique reflections of Christ. Lighthouse leaders multiply other leaders who stand tall as examples and light the way with their mentoring, compassion, generosity, and empowerment.

Are you a lighthouse leader? Are you committed to having the heart and the humility to lead with the compassion and clarity of Jesus? Have you surrendered yourself to a mission so great that the only option is to lead in this way?

Our world is on the lookout for leaders who are willing to challenge the status quo, set a new standard, and model a pattern of leadership that was first defined in the Gospels with

Jesus, the Light of the World.[1] Every lighthouse leader follows that pattern:

- they have clarity of mission,
- they are teachers and mentors,
- they are compassionate,
- they are clear,
- they are generous, and
- they are empowering.

If you know a lighthouse leader, I want you to remember that they weren't born that way. They may possess some natural giftings, and if they are believers, the fruit of the Spirit equips and empowers them. But as believers, the most important thing each of them did was commit him- or herself to developing Jesus' easy-to-follow behaviors and disciplining themselves to demonstrate them consistently. Some of the most impactful people in our lives have been hard at work mastering these skills for years; others have remained focused on growth for decades, all for the sake of others.

That's why I find the term *personal growth* an oxymoron. When a person commits to growth, everyone who has a relationship with them enjoys the benefits of their efforts. As you commit to learn, grow, and change into an easy-to-follow leader, your "personal growth" becomes both inspirational and influential to countless others. You and I have the God-given opportunity to become beacons directing people to their destinations and ensuring their safety along the journey of leadership and life.

I leave you with some of Jesus' words to his disciples:

"You are the light of the world. A town built on a hill cannot be hidden. Neither do people light a lamp and put it under a bowl. Instead they put it on its stand, and it gives light to everyone in the house. In the same way, let your light shine before others, that they may see your good deeds and glorify your Father in heaven."[2]

You might be the only lighthouse someone ever sees. So shine brightly like Christ, and become an easy-to-follow leader.

I've had seasons in my leadership journey when I've been easy to follow and seasons when I've been difficult. To keep me on track, I put together a ten-question "easy to follow" diagnostic that will quickly tell me whether I am being easy to follow and what I should work on if not. If that interests you, use this QR code to learn more. You've come this far and asked a lot of hard questions, so now's the time to take one more step in your leadership journey.

Acknowledgments

To my wife, Ronda: I know of no human being easier to follow than you. Your selfless heart, your empathy, and your generosity are all examples of how deeply Christ dwells in you.

To my friend and coauthor, Kat: You are the reason this book exists. From the moment you heard the origins of the *Easy to Follow* concepts, you relentlessly and passionately made this work a reality. Thank you for the lessons you've taught me and the leadership you've modeled in this process.

To our Integrus team: Your influence and fingerprints are all over the pages of this book. Your feedback has shaped this narrative, and your lives have inspired me to become a better leader, friend, and follower of Jesus. Thank you for teaching others how to be easy to follow.

To the team at NavPress: You have been vital in crafting this story and creating this resource. I thank you for your clarity, constructive critique, and passion for this project.

Finally, to all the leaders who have modeled these concepts for me: Your leadership and lessons taught me what it means to truly be easy to follow.

Resources for Leaders

FREE ASSESSMENT
Start with a five-minute assessment to discover your leadership style.

30-DAY PRAYER GUIDE
Use the thirty-day prayer guide for spiritual growth.

DIGITAL COURSE
Go deeper with a five-session digital course on becoming an easy-to-follow leader.

Integrus Leadership Resources

EXECUTIVE COACHING

Integrus Leadership specializes in monthly online, one-on-one behavioral leadership coaching for Kingdom-minded leaders. Integrus's executive coaching includes an Integrus360 profile (a leadership assessment tool), a customized growth plan, and real-time support.

LEADERSHIP BREAKTHROUGH

Leadership Breakthrough is an in-person or online one-day workshop that develops healthy leaders and effective teams. Leadership Breakthrough includes Integrus360 profiles for all your team members and a customized action plan designed to leverage their unique strengths.

LEADERSHIP PATHWAY

Leadership Pathway is a six-part leadership-development program that you can experience in three, six, or twelve months either in person or online. Starting with the Five-Day Leader Workshop, the program proceeds with live ninety-minute sessions that emphasize practical tools over inspirational quotes or abstract theories, making it ideal for leaders and teams seeking tangible leadership development that lasts.

About the Authors

Lyle Wells is the president of Integrus Leadership; the senior pastor at First Baptist Franklin, Texas; an elite executive coach to hundreds of Kingdom-minded leaders; and the author of *The Five-Day Leader: An Insanely Practical Guide for Relentless Growth, Ridiculous Routines, and Resilient Relationships*. Lyle's ministry experience includes serving as a church planter and an executive senior pastor at one of the largest churches in the nation. Lyle spent decades transforming athletic programs and serving as a leader in higher education. His passion on the basketball court and for his teams is matched only by his fervor for healthy ministry leaders who accelerate their Kingdom impact. Lyle is a devoted husband and present father. He has been married to Ronda for thirty-six years, and together they love creating spontaneous family fun for their two grown children, Michael and Jordie. Lyle's a golf and basketball enthusiast and enjoys a cold Dr Pepper, a greasy burger, and sizzling fajitas.

lylewells.com   integrus.org
@leadwithlyle   @integrusleadership

Kat Armstrong was born in Houston, Texas, where the humidity ruins her Mexi-German curls. She is a powerful voice in our generation as a sought-after Bible teacher, preacher, and leader, and she's on a mission to spark holy curiosity in a generation of Bible readers. She holds a master's degree from Dallas Theological Seminary and is pursuing a doctorate of ministry in New Testament context. Kat is the author of *No More Holding Back*; *The In-Between Place*; and an eight-book Bible study series, the **Storyline Bible Studies**, as well as the cofounder of the Polished Network and the host of the *Holy Curiosity* podcast. She and her husband, Aaron, have been married for over twenty years; live in McKinney, Texas, with their son, Caleb; and attend the church in McKinney where Aaron serves as the lead pastor.

katarmstrong.com
@katarmstrong1

thestorylineproject.com
@thestorylineproject

Notes

ONE | JESUS IS EASY TO FOLLOW
1. John 1:34.
2. John 1:41.
3. John 1:49; Revelation 19:16.

TWO | JESUS CLEARLY DEFINED HIS MISSION
1. "Rick Warren," Simon & Schuster, accessed February 6, 2025, https://www.simonandschuster.com/authors/Rick-Warren/39904606.
2. Erwin W. Lutzer, "John Harper's Last Convert," Moody Church Media, accessed March 17, 2025, https://www.moodymedia.org/articles/sharing-gift-christmas-one-minute-you-die.
3. Kat Armstrong, *Sinners: Experiencing Jesus' Compassion in the Middle of Your Sin, Struggles, and Shame* (Colorado Springs: NavPress, 2023), 10.
4. Armstrong, *Sinners*, 11.
5. Jordan K. Monson, "The Woman Who Gave the World a Thousand Names for God: How a British Linguist and a Failed Nigerian Coup Changed Everything about Bible Translation," *Christianity Today*, October 2022, https://www.christianitytoday.com/2022/10/linguist-katharine-barnwell-bible-translation-Jesus-film.
6. Luke 2:49, NLT.
7. "38% of U.S. Pastors Have Thought about Quitting Full-Time Ministry in the Past Year," Barna, November 16, 2021, https://www.barna.com/research/pastors-well-being.

8. "Poll Results: Stress and Burnout Pose Threat of Educator Shortages," National Education Association, January 31, 2022, https://www.nea.org/sites/default/files/2022-02/NEA%20Member%20COVID-19%20Survey%20Summary.pdf.
9. Matthew 12:48.
10. Theodore Roosevelt, "Citizenship in a Republic," speech, April 23, 1910, Sorbonne, Paris, "The Man in the Arena," Theodore Roosevelt Center, Dickinson State University, https://www.theodorerooseveltcenter.org/Learn-About-TR/TR-Encyclopedia/Culture-and-Society/Man-in-the-Arena.aspx.

THREE | JESUS TAUGHT HIS METHODS; HE DIDN'T JUST TELL THEM

1. See Juliana Menasce Horowitz and Kim Parker, "How Americans View Their Jobs," Pew Research Center, March 30, 2023, https://www.pewresearch.org/social-trends/2023/03/30/how-americans-view-their-jobs.
2. *Turn the other cheek*: Matthew 5:39; *care for the poor*: Luke 12:33-34; *let their light shine*: Matthew 5:14-16.
3. Matthew 21:12-13.
4. John 8:12.
5. Matthew 16:13, 15.
6. Matthew 28:18-20.

FOUR | JESUS MENTORED, NOT MANAGED, HIS TEAM

1. Matthew 16:24, NRSV.
2. Matthew 10:6-8.

FIVE | JESUS PRACTICED UNCOMMON COMPASSION

1. "Have pity"; "have (be moved with) compassion"; "deep empathy"; "to feel the bowels yearn." Logos Bible Software, s.v. "σπλαγχνίζομαι (*splanchnizomai*)," accessed June 10, 2025.
2. Luke 7:11-12.
3. Luke 7:13, NRSV.
4. Luke 7:15, NRSV.
5. Proverbs 14:12, NLT.
6. Proverbs 18:1, NRSV.
7. Proverbs 26:12, HCSB.
8. Proverbs 27:5.
9. Proverbs 27:17.
10. Mark 1:41, KJV.
11. Mark 1:41.

12. James 2:1, CSB.
13. Matthew 9:36, NLT.
14. John 8:11, NLT.

SIX | JESUS CLARIFIED HIS EXPECTATIONS

1. Brené Brown, *Dare to Lead: Brave Work. Tough Conversations. Whole Hearts.* (New York: Random House, 2018), 48.
2. Matthew 5:3-12.

SEVEN | JESUS CULTIVATED GENEROSITY

1. "Over 2 in 5 U.S. Adults Have at Least One Unused Gift Card, Totaling About $27 Billion," Bankrate, September 23, 2024, https://www.bankrate.com/f/102997/x/c53caa68d4/gift-card-survey-press-release.pdf.
2. "Bad Customer Service Interactions More Likely to Be Shared than Good Ones," Marketing Charts, April 15, 2013, https://www.marketingcharts.com/digital-28628.
3. Philippians 2:5-6, CSB.
4. John Wooden with Jack Tobin, *They Call Me Coach* (Chicago: Contemporary Books, 2004), 146.
5. Philippians 2:8.

EIGHT | JESUS EMPOWERED OTHERS

1. "Men's Basketball: Mike Krzyzewski," Duke Athletics, updated May 6, 2025, https://goduke.com/sports/mens-basketball/roster/coaches/mike-krzyzewski/533.
2. Quoted in Don Yaeger, "Duke Legend Mike Krzyzewski to Leaders, 'Your Team Won't Own It Until They Feel It,'" *Forbes*, November 8, 2023, https://www.forbes.com/sites/donyaeger/2023/11/08/duke-legend-mike-krzyzewski-to-leaders-your-team-wont-own-it-until-they-feel-it.
3. Matthew 14:16.
4. Matthew 10:14, CSB.
5. Matthew 28:20.
6. Matthew 28:19.

A FINAL QUESTION | ARE YOU EASY TO FOLLOW?

1. John 8:12.
2. Matthew 5:14-16.

Storyline Bible Studies
by Kat Armstrong

Each study follows people, places, or things throughout the Bible. This approach allows you to see the cohesive storyline of Scripture and appreciate the Bible as the literary masterpiece that it is.

Access free resources to help you teach or lead a small group at thestorylineproject.com.

NavPress   STORYLINE